The Bitch Left

By

David Simpson

1stBooks - rev. 06/17/13

Introduction.

You might start wonder to why you have bought this book. The simple answer is that you are in some trouble getting to grips with the fact that the one true love of your life has left you. Why did she? What was it that you did to make her leave you? Will she come back?

These are probably the questions that you are asking yourself and wondering how you got into this mess. Everything was going fine in your life. You had everything that you could want and you loved her beyond belief. Now that she has gone you find yourself in the depths of despair.

So now you have reached out for anything that will give you some help finding your answer. I found myself exactly where you are and wished that there was something like this book to have helped me find some answers to the same questions. When I couldn't find anything to help I thought that I would try and do it myself. It is not an easy thing to do, putting your inner most feelings down on paper as it can be embarrassing but I do this for a good reason. I found that It helped me get over the problems that I was going through with the breakup of my marriage.

Writing this book was almost like therapy and surprisingly, at the end of it all it made me feel a lot better. Everything that I have written in this book is completely honest and true. I tried to explain through words how I felt when it all happened which is very difficult to do. To make people understand just how bad you felt at that time is damn near impossible. Unless you are actually going through the same thing or have done in the past, you wont be able to imagine the same sort of emotional pain and torture that these problems give you. It all seems a bit doom and gloom when someone spells it out for you like that, but this is rightly so as you probably feel like shit and your head is upside down with you worry everyday about how you will get through this. There are lucky people out there who do not understand how you could have got in such a state over a woman. Well fortunately or unfortunately we are not all alike. But still have a read and be happier knowing that others do feel as you do now. Anyway this is how it all came about:

The Idea.

Whilst walking around in a bookstore in Memphis, my girlfriend was looking for a book to give her friend as a gift to help cheer her up after her divorce, she was looking at books with titles such as "Life after him"......and "We don't need men"....or something to that demeaning effect, cataloguing men as the root of all evil when it comes to the break up of relationships.........!

Admittedly though if you look back over the past few decades then it has always appeared that Men did in fact dish out the crap when it came to the end of a relationship. It was the done thing, he would just announce that he didn't have any interest in her any more, swing his coat over his shoulder and then walk out the front door leaving the Woman in tears

1

screaming after him that she loves him and always will….but her words would fall on deaf ears as he just calmly walks off into the night. It was the Manly way to do it, anything else just wasn't done, I mean we couldn't have men admitting that they actually LOVED someone could we, that just wasn't how it was done. I learned on my travels through the Middle East that their way of thinking is still pretty much back there with our cavemen. For instance to get divorced an Arab just has to say,

"I divorce thee, I divorce thee, I divorce thee" and hey presto he is divorced and the woman gets nothing.

However in the real World I do believe that things are changing, so the question that Men can feel brave enough to ask now is….

What about the way that MEN feel when it happens to us? …… by that I mean when our wives or girlfriends leave us! Contrary to main belief, MEN DO CRY…… and in my case I think that I cried enough for a life-time in that 12 month period when my wife decided to leave me…….!

Many women reading the last paragraph might laugh and stand united for the feminist movement and be the first to shout

"who gives a Shit about the way you MEN feel, you've been treating us women like crap for years".

Some men probably have indeed been treating women like crap for years, however ladies there are a few decent Men out there who do love their partners and would do anything for them. I know that many of you might find that a disturbing and a disbelieving idea that MEN are capable of love, but I'm sure you'll find it one day, and that is not meant to be condescending in anyway he really is out there.

So because of what happened to me I decided then, whilst thinking how unfair it was that I couldn't see any books on the subject of how we feel after the WOMAN leaves, to set my experience down on paper.....not in the hope of gaining a great fortune if this book ever gets published, (although money in vast amounts is always nice) but in the hope that it might help other's in the world who have to go through the same pain as me....and help them get through it...because while you have to go through it you feel that no-one in the world has ever felt this bad when a relationship ends, and that no-one could ever feel anywhere near as bad as you...I want to just assure you that they have, they do and they always will.

All that I do hope is that it does help you see that everything will one day be ok....it takes a long time to forget and some say that you will never get over it, but the pain does ease.....slowly.....very slowly...and perhaps you do not want to believe it right now especially if it is happening to you ...but it will. In some small ways you don't want the pain to end because you know that it will only stop when one of two things happen, one is that you get back together and live happily ever after and never look back on what has happened, or the other is that you know you'll never get back together and will have completely finished.

It's a very thin line in your mind and you fear crossing it in case it's the wrong answer. I hope for your sake that you cross the line and get the answer that you need. Emotional problems can't be fixed by anyone else or by anything else. Some take pills some have therapy, they work for some people and they don't for others. I decided not to do either. I knew that I had to find a way out of this for myself because the pills and the therapy will only last so long and can't be there forever. So I decided to go it alone,

This is my story of what happened to me!……………..

WHAT IS LOVE = *Love, luv, N. Fondness: Charity: affection of the mind caused by that which delights: Strong liking: devoted attachment to one of the opposite sex :sexual attachment love affair :the object of affection :used as a term of endearment or affection: the God of love Cupid, Eros: a kindness, a favour done(shak) the mear pleasure of playing without stakes: in some games no score-v.t. to be fond of: to regard with affection :to delight in with exclusive affection: to regard with benevolence-V.I. to have the feeling of love (full dictionary explanation)*

In The Beginning?

I have vague recollections of being hurt by girlfriends since I first took an interest in the Female race, but it seems that MEN never learn the true power that Women have over us emotionally. It is a grave misconception that the Stereotypical male is invincible from emotional hurt. Whilst on the outside he is a stony faced bastard who doesn't give a shit about "Her" feelings, inside he is being torn apart and will have to wait for a moment alone to come to terms with his own emotions and eventually let that pain out. These days though I believe that all men are realising that its ok to show emotion and pain, and it is showing through that some of us are releasing our emotions and therefore showing that Men can be subject to actually having some feelings. I know that this will horrify most men who hear of this yet there are some of us who have decided that its about time others knew how we felt.

Going back to the Cavemen days when men were supposedly the dominant race. We would go out into the hills club the first female we saw over the head and then drag her back to our cave and take full sexual advantage of her in her semi-conscious state. After fulfilling our sexual appetite with what we believed to be our God-given rite, I mean why else would he put women on the earth? We would then expect them to cook, wash and clean forever after tending to our every need and never raise their voice and perform sexual acts whenever we desired, which is usually every hour without complaint, and they had to remain loyal to us even though we would perform the same ritual with everyother breathing female that we could find in a twenty mile radius. Women seem to think that things haven't changed very much over the ages and still label us Men as Cavemen and Neanderthals etc...

In the woman's defence there are men out there who still act as though they were cavemen out hunting for their next victim. You have only got to look down a busy high street when the pubs close to see evidence of this. And a herd of drunken young males is not a pretty site, this we notice when rarely sober and walking through a town centre. What is there excuse? Well do they need one? It's just the male way isn't it? Go out drink as much as you can without throwing up. Stagger from pub to pub taunting the women. Trying to get lucky and find one who is interested in you and then buy her drinks all night in the hope that your conversation will turn into something a little more physical. Although if you have ever seen a hen night out on the town in action you will have noticed that they can be just the same if not a bit worse than the men.

Maybe it is that Men just have this dysfunction of never being able to show emotional pain or even talk about how emotions can affect us…. This may have been true when we walked the earth and clubbed all the Women, but I think that over these passed ages we have begun to have Male equality on the subject of love and I think that it is time to forget the stature that we are supposed to remain as hard as our forefathers and learn to understand that we can be caring and loving and considerate towards women after all its nothing to be ashamed of. We all do it in the comfort of our own homes out of sight of our friends so why not allow that into everyday life?

Course there are some who do show their feelings constantly in front of others. Sometimes though it is almost too much and they try to overcompensate to show everyone that they love her. This covers up the fact that can rarely do it with feelings. Yet this is the way that you try and express your love.

We all have different ways I guess.

I mean its not as if women don't like it. You will receive far more from a relationship if you are completely honest. Yet men still have a problem with those three little words. (I love you). Of course you cant just keep saying it all the time, you have to make sure that it is said at the right moment and that you don't say it because you think she needs to hear it.

On the down side though this new found emotion that we have uncovered in the male genetics recently has resulted in 'Us' the men of the World also being able to feel the immense pain that is struck throughout our entire body when a loved one decides rightly or wrongly that we are no longer their life partner, and simply say's

"I don't love you anymore, and I don't think that we should see each-other ……"!

Oh on the surface immediately we will pretend that it doesn't matter and that we will just move on to the next conquest. Some Men from the old school are like that. There is no doubt a physiological explanation about the fact that if they were unloved as a child receiving hardly any tactile emotion that it would make us an unemotional bastard as some women might say, but there are others who suffer with huge amounts of pain when someone we love goes.

So when the Female's now tell us were no longer required it stir's feeling's that 'Us' men are not used to. We were always thought of as the cold-hearted bastards that break off a relationship without suffering any consequences. After all in our animal kingdom it is the Alpha male makes all the decisions…doesn't he?

Are we not the ones who should provide and protect the family and be loved beyond all belief by that said family and held up high, respected by all outsiders too?

I think that is how we were perceived in the 60's maybe but now things have moved on and the Alpha male is slowly loosing his grip on the reigns of the relationships and that colder than ice appearance that we have is definitely melting away.

We are slowly learning that Women prefer the softer man, the caring and loveable character that they have all dreamt off whilst listening to tales of old and watching Snow White or some new romantic film that portrays the man as a very caring and loveable creature. The problem is though that most of 'Us' men in the world still believe that we are the same as our forefathers were two generations back and insist that MEN are MEN I'm sure that we can all relate to that belief and remembering our grandfathers they were from the days when Men worked very long hours in jobs that required sheer strength all day and would spend most of the night down the club. It really was a man's world back then.

We have all seen the films where the male is the strong handsome stranger that rides into town on his horse claiming the hearts of all the town's women, believing that we too are desired by every female that we have eye contact with. We all secretly wanted to be him.

We still to this day have the idea that we are Clint Eastwood. Yet now the reality is slowly beginning to make us men cower and unwillingly accept that things have definitely changed. NO, NO I hear you shout, but unfortunately we have to admit that we are becoming more in touch with our feminine sides. Now hold on don't panic that doesn't mean that we all are going to soon be wearing dresses and thongs, although if that's one mans certain thing then I have nothing bad to say about that, I mean each to his own. What I is mean we have all seen our girlfriends behind in a thong and some of those are wearing them clearly for comfort so they say but knowingly they are fully aware of how good it looks, but come on imagine a man's big fat hairy arse hanging out of one!!!! Not a pretty sight really I think you'll have to imagine.

Problem is we don't want to change just yet, were still clinging to the good old days and when a girl tells us that it's over we think, what how dare you do that to me! When we were all younger in our teens we would usually say something really stupid like 'well I was going to finish with you anyway', or 'well your boobs are to small so you saved me the problem of ditching you'…But I think that only happens in pre-pubescence love though…believe me if you're a young reader and trying to get some insight into love and relationships then things definitely get a little more difficult after that stage of our life, I can honestly say that. Don't be put off by that though as it is a great way to learn.

But for God's sake don't rush those pre-puberty relationships, as they are the foundations of what is going to happen to you in the next few years. Enjoy those years of idolising the sexiest girl in school only to be rejected with every advance that you make, the pretence that you don't care when she ignores you or laughs at you. This is where is all begins. Yes it hurts and deflates your ego for a while but ten minutes later you realise that its her friend that you fancy really so don't worry its all a good learning curve for you.

You will learn as you enter into relationships, emotions are extremely difficult to control. In fact they are impossible. You can't make yourself like someone even if others do. They either fit or don't fit into your complex world. People have studied human behaviour in all aspects and come up with many different conclusions as to why we all act in different ways. I personally thought that was purely because we are made up of different values. Our up bringing and surroundings I believe have a lot to do with a person's manner. There is no doubt that we are either like someone in our family, that is just purely biological and fortunately or unfortunately there is nothing that we can do about that.

It has been proved that for some crazy reason's opposites attract. We end up falling for the one that textbooks say we shouldn't.

Therefore we are what we are, and short of copious amounts of drugs and electroshock therapy we will remain. So in this we have to accept what we are and how we react to different emotional hurdles. These hurdles always seem to appear when we least expect them. Its usually when you think everything is going fine and then SMACK, there's a hurdle to get over. Yet all that we can do is keep jumping.

What I have written is just how I have seen things and dealt with them from my point of view as it has all been forced upon me. You just have to accept it and try somehow to come to terms with it. There is no right or wrong way that we handle it. We have to just do the as best we are able given the way our emotions make us feel. Women certainly put us to the test. Its bloody good fun learning all this stuff when you're young and first start realising that women are more than they appear. However a word to the wise, it all gets very complicated as you get older, so enjoy young love. It will break your heart and it will make you very happy.

Your Preparation:

The problem with the fairer sex, is that you're not really sure when your feelings towards them are going to change. We have to understand exactly what women are for in life. They are not just objects of desire as we have all seen them. They are sensitive people just like us. Although they are incredibly different in their views on the perfect life we are all searching for the same things. We have to learn to love them for what they can give us back in a relationship. We have to understand that they need us as much as we need them and we have to respect that. We have to find a level ground where we all compromise and get the best out of a partnership. The fundamental role of humans is to mate and reproduce, but there is so much more to it. Growing together with each other is all a part of that togetherness that we all crave. When we do fall in love we have no warnings either, nobody takes you to one side and lets you know that you're about to start having weird feelings about girls, it just happens. They are no longer 'Just one of the boys'. You notice other things about their presence…and you actually start to like it and the way they make you feel. They change toward you and you know something is going on…well hold on to your hat because now your in trouble…this is where is all starts getting interesting….

I'm sure that we can all remember the first time that our heart's were broken, in my case I was on a school trip to the Isle of White and I for some time had really liked this girl in my class and believed that she was the most beautiful girl in the world…well for that week anyway. It started the usual way that primary school relationships start with calling her Fat or Ugly, you remember those wonderful characteristics that we think shows the affection that we have for the female, maybe even a bit of stone throwing at break time, yes now she really understand that I truly loved her because she threw one back and then started crying, that meant that I had her emotionally bound to me for the rest of her life…this began a new wave of emotions that I had never before even thought about, where have these come from.

At first your not really sure how to react inside, I mean you can't go over and just start talking to her…. what would your friends think. Imagine the crap that they will give me for talking to a 'Girl'!

However realising that her love for me was undying by the throwing back of my stone I purchased at great expense of 25p a badge in the shape of a heart with her name on it and little flowers. Then in true romantic style I plucked up enough courage and asked one of her close friends to give it to her. Feeling pleased with myself after offering her this token of my love at the end of the week on the coach ride home, I sat there feeling very happy with myself, I sat waiting the response to this offering and found butterflies stirring in my stomach.

This again was a new set of feelings that were rushing around in my head. Picturing her sat there gazing lovingly at the gift and then in my direction trying to pluck up the courage herself to come over and thank me with a look or if I was really lucky a hold of the hand. I began to enjoy these thoughts of us together sitting there holding hands on the journey home, thinking of what we should say and do, love is a truly wonderful experience I thought, I like this a lot. I can't say really that this was love as I was very young. I just know that I felt different inside for the first time, something that I had never felt before. Butterflies were stirring up in my stomach as I saw her talking to her friend about my tremendous gift and they were giggling about it. This is a good sign I thought and soon she would come over and say thank you for the gift.

The feelings inside my stomach got worse and I realised that there was far more to life than action men, bikes and play fights. This was weird but good.

These new wondrous feelings however were short-lived and I realised this as her friend returned shortly and handed me the badge back saying that she didn't want it as Richard was now her Boyfriend and that he wouldn't like it! Devastated wasn't the word, I probably didn't even know that word yet but the feeling of my insides were being stamped all over I think gave me the same kind of message as to being devastated.

Resisting the urge to go and confront Richard and kick him in the balls I decided to sit there and ignore the returned gift and act as if I wasn't that bothered. Well that was the plan for the next few seconds until I had the strangest feeling which I had never had before in the pit of my stomach, a kind of sick feeling…then I felt a complete lack of control and become a gibbering crying wreck in full view of everyone else on the coach instead.

I was very surprised though to have the support of my elder sister who happened to be on the trip and she simply went and told her what a little cow she was. God what a day, first I fall in what I think is love and then learn how quickly it can all be taken away. This may have had irretrievable effects on me for the rest of my life.

It is strange how we learn that in our hours of emotional need the sibling rivalry that normally keeps the fighting constant, stops for that short time and they help you through it. The thing is though it isn't too long before that magic is lost and your back screaming at each other, kicking, punching and completely denying it when our parents tried to be the referee. Despite all of the fighting and backstabbing over the years you realise that your family are simply the best support for you in times of emotional crisis and they are truly wonderful at it. Why is it that they are so good at it? Well its simply because they sit there and listen and tell you all the things that you want to hear such as "She wasn't good enough for you anyway, you can do much better than that". Families are a very funny and they do unexpected things constantly yet they are the people who you can always rely on.

Pre-pubescence life is a very difficult time, wondering why we liked girls one-minute and then after your first initial scare with the Female race we then leave them alone for some considerable years and only occasionally may have a crush on a girl at school because it was cool, and it also stopped the playground gangs from chanting your "Gay" in the playground. This was often dependant on weather you were accepted into the class gang that particular day by the 'cool' guy who everyone seemed to want to be. That has probably bought back some good and bad memories for you.

I mean come on you remember him... the cool bastard that always had the most perfect life, everyone wanted to be him...he would set the way and the trends but if you didn't follow him them you were either one of the five nerds that always just hung out with eachother and played cards wearing your free glasses. The gang would have bets on which ones would end up being Gay, or you were the underprivileged kids that got free school meals because they didn't have much money, or one of the compulsory third groups of people that were just hated constantly, this group always had some poor little thing with ginger hair and freckles with his national health black glasses, that poor sod was in for a rough ride for the rest of his schooling. But you know now that he is probably the next Bill Gates or something like that.

Then we slowly entered in to puberty where everything in our lives begin to change and we learn new things everyday about the main thing in the world that women believe we rule our lives by SEX. Yes SEX and lots of it...oh yeah I have SEX all of the time? Well that's the image that has been portrayed to us all since we could watch films, our all action heroes always ends up getting the gorgeous women, and so shall we. We find our perfect hero weather it be a film star or a pop star whatever is the in thing at the time. We aspire to become them.

This usually means a trip to the barbers to get the haircut which we think makes us look like them, buying the fashion accessory earring, the continuous stances in front of our mothers full length mirror when everyone was out to get that stance and look just right, and then there is the ceremonial shaving off of those two nurtured blonde hairs on our chin and then finally go and find ourselves a woman just like in the films…

Yeah then we wake up…because we learn a cruel lesson at a young age that those things only do happen in the films unless of course you were that cool bastard from primary school that is still adored by every living women in history. However undeterred we deal with these hurdles in our stride and with us still wanting to be that 'cool guy'. We love to hate him, yet want to be him so much. All the girls go on about him and will only talk to you if you know him. It paints a bad picture for us but we have all don't it. It takes a lot of courage to be an individual at a young age as most of the time the individuals just get ridiculed and end up attaching themselves to the nerd group and befriend the ginger haired kid with the national health glasses.

But a word to the wise about our old friend Mr Cool, his days of being the loved celebrity through school don't last that long once school and puberty are over. He gets his comeuppance later on in his early twenties; you end up out somewhere one night with some friends and stumble into a distance face from the past at the bar. You search your memory as you think that there is something about him that you recognise, you cant quite put your finger on it yet there is something about this person. Something is niggling in the back of your mind!

But what is it? Do you know him? Should you know him…. its really starting to bug you now and Then he speaks to you and says,

"Hi, you don't remember me do you?"

"You know I don't, but feel that I should, you are familiar" and your not lying because you still haven't figured out whom it is yet.

Then he finally says,

"Its me John from primary school,. John Harper, remember me we were in the same class?

You think for a minute and study this face in front of you, there is something familiar but what…? you just cant place that face. Then all of a sudden it all comes flooding back. At once you are biting your lip and say,

"God yes, how are you I didn't recognise you!" You feel a burning desire to laugh at the fact that Mr Cool has turned into a bald spotty faced fat bastard. You just want to relish in the fact that he has turned out like this. You stand their admiring your discovery and want to remind him of how it was for you at school with him taking all the available women…oh ha so where are they now Fatty you want to shout.

You make idle chit chat until you have been served your drink's and are able to return to your friends and tell them all about what just happened. This is divine retribution and you wished that the whole class could see him now. The best part of this long awaited surprise is that he is now going out with a fat ugly girl that you would only think about one night stand with in sheer desperation, it's truly a feeling that is worth waiting 10 years for I can tell you. Some of you will read this and then one day bump into Mr Cool yourself and then remember reading this and only then agree at how wonderful it feels. Unless of course you are that Mr Cool! In which case go and look in the mirror now!!

Then the moment that you have been waiting for and thinking about hits you when you least expect it and you look your worst, staggering about with your shirt hanging out and singing Suspicious minds completely out of tune after drinking a few sips of the bottle of whisky that you stole from your Dads drink cabinet.... You meet a sweet little girl and everything in the world changes. It hits you like a train out of nowhere. You attempt to stand up straight and deny all allegations from her that you are a little drunk and try a conversation.

You gaze into her general direction and just keep staring trying to smile. (God if only you could see the state that your in). Oh shit then you remember that huge zit on your chin and try to conceal it by speaking with your hand in front of your mouth.

This always ends with her smiling sweetly and informing you that she had to go home, as she was already late. Out of no where you suddenly find yourself asking her if she had a boyfriend, and if she didn't would she like to go out with you…The pause in conversation that follows seems to go on for an eternity, you question your own stupidity as to why you asked her now, you hardly know her and then nerves begin to make you convince yourself that she will laugh and tell you to drop dead, yet all the time there is the tiniest of hope that she might actually say yes to you…. again the suspense is killing you and your also dying for the loo! Will she wont she? ..You're trying to still look and seem sober but know that your efforts are going to let you down. With that she walks forward and smiles and says….

"Get stuffed you drunken tosser" well that is what you think she is going to say but what you hear is

"I'd like that, do you have a pen and I'll give you my number"

You frantically dart into the nearest Kebab shop pleading the Greek man behind the counter for a pen inside knowing that you'll give him whatever he wants for it. Finally you manage to scrawl down the number say your goodbyes and clutch onto that piece of paper for your life on the way home.

The changes and reactions that a female can enforce on a man unbeknown to her, happens overnight. You change immediately and a new chapter in your life begins. The day that Mothers all over the world dream of and you actually enjoy taking a bath and spending more time than your sister getting ready to go out. Personal hygiene actually becomes reality and also becomes part of your daily routines and you begin to clean your teeth every couple of hours.

If all this change isn't hard enough already you have to try to ignore the elder brother and sister chants of "he's got a girlfriend ooohhhh". You need to look like Mr Cool from school, you change you walk you hair your appearance so many times in reality you get a little self obsessed. Upon leaving the house for your first date you respond to the chants from the upstairs window

"Get lost and don't be stupid," you shout back as you become so embarrassed and happy all at the same time because as you think to yourself hey I do have a girlfriend and she is gorgeous. You feel brave enough to even mouth the words "F***OFF" to them as you cant let your parents hear you say that, they'd kill you.

So you start the dating game and all is going fine. You realise that girls are fun as they make you feel better about yourself and life. There is nothing like a good woman to life your spirits. The trouble is though when things are going well you sometimes think that it's all going too well. This is where paranoia sets in. After a while you start worrying that she is losing interest or fancies your best friend more, so you start trying to change the way you are towards her. You begin to purchase little gifts for her spending all of your money on flowers and slushy cards confessing your undying love for her and always act so coy about it when asked by your friends if you have shagged her yet? This is always the first question that they want answered, they don't care if you actually like her, or if she is nice they just want to know all about the nitty gritty of sex. This is probably as they haven't had sex yet and have only pretended to of done it. They fact is though when they ask you that dreaded questions you are very embarrassed by the fact that you still haven't really kissed her properly, its not like the ugly ones that you snogged at the school discos this one is special and you want to take things slowly.

So weeks then turn into a couple off months and you have gone through all of the young love foreplay acts together and are trying to find an approach to the SEX thing. You always find though that one of your friends has done the Sex thing with more than one girl. He then becomes Mr Cool and everybody wants to know what its like? How long did it last? Was it as good as he expected? Of course he would tell the crowd of sheep what they wanted to hear and we would hang on his every word. Chances are you find out years later that he was still a virgin at that stage and just wanted to be Mr Cool for a while. Sad but true, still it made him feel better about his acne didn't it! But being male's we cant get that thought of SEX out of our head and think that the only way we can really become a Man is to have sex. Where has this mentality come from? God only knows, but we know that having sex gives lots of pleasure and allows us to have control of a situation.

That is a poor view of it, but there are probably thousands of ways to analyse the fact that men just love sex. Maybe its also a power thing, what I mean by that is, women cant give sex to men, men have to give sex to the women. I mean fairs fair; god gave women breasts and men penises. Which ever way that you do look at it though men overtime have given themselves a bad name by sleeping with as many women as they can. I think though that even these statistics are becoming into balance with women having just as much if not more partners than men. I think there is still this poor view of society that if women sleep around they are sluts or slags, yet if men sleep around they are a real catch, Mr stud… Personally if you are happy and enjoy it then sleep with as many people as you want. As long as people are happy and no body gets hurt then what is the problem?

The Sex thing is always tricky when young, well it was in my days as a teenager, it seems these days that if you're a virgin at 15 you're the odd one out. Thankfully though over the decades are whole view on sex has changed and become more liberal and that allows us to talk about sex and the delights and dangers that it can bring us. People are defiantly having more sex in this day and age than in our parents younger days.

Sex for the first time when you were going through puberty was always something that you dreamt about, something for those quiet times when your alone as a young male masturbating yourself into the unconscious dream land that every young boy goes through. What did we do pre erections? I bet you cant remember can you? A stupid dream about fighting with the incredible hulk was probably all we could imagine, being the superhero that eventually won. Oh how simple life was as a child. But we have to agree that it was a glorious day finally learning what your penis was for. That's the day that every boy believes that he as becoming a man. Well only in the sense that we knew it gave us enormous pleasure when we used it ourselves.

We would joke about it with friends at school, at least we finally knew what a Wanker was even though we'd been calling each other it for the past few years. Its funny how we used to talk about it quite innocently with our friends at school and openly discuss the latest new girl that we had all heard about and couldn't wait to see. I know that men still talk about their sexual antics amongst others of the same pride. Its very animalistic isn't it the men discussing how it was how she was, what she would let him do. Whereas the gentle women would sit around whilst discussing their haircuts and the latest nail polish or makeup.

At least that is what we believed but you know that that was very naive of us don't you ladies. Women talking to women are probably far more detailed in explaining exactly what happens in the bedroom. They will explain every movement and feeling that they went through and describe them. Men however just point out the bare hard face facts,

"Yeah I shagged her, she gave me a great blow job and then I fell asleep!!!!"

I know that its not like that all of the time and probably was different, but other men don't want to know all the details. If they did then I think you should watch who your talking too!!!!!

Although to this day there is one sexual experience that is still taboo for men to mention. Men don't mention their masturbating activities with complete honesty. Ask a man if he wanks and watch how uncomfortable he gets. He may shock you and answer honestly but most just like to ignore the question. Why? It is the unknown territories of our bedroom and of course if ever asked if we masturbate we reply in a shocked response 'NO' with guilt written all over. Oh and please don't sit there reading this book and deny all knowledge of doing it yourself. It is one of those unexplained phenomena's that no man has ever masturbated, past the age of sixteen. Lets just get one thing straight if you pardon the pun, we have all done it and always have done and will continue to do so until the days when it doesn't work anymore. Even then though we can now thank Mr Scientist for inventing Viagra. Although many men will say that its only the single poor bastard's that actually wank, many married men still on the odd chance they get like to go back to basic's when alone and remember the good old days of just dick and him.

I asked four drunken friends who all have wives or long term partners if they still had a wank..Of course I do said Mr T, but he's always up front about life and never lies. It's just something that I enjoy and therefore I will continue to do it!! Actually this was pretty much the same answer from all four of the men who agreed that even though sex was great and being with their partner was wonderful they still had the need for a quick one all alone in the bathroom.

We soon realise during foreplay that when women take their turn at masturbating us it just clearly isn't the same. You may experience one or two that come close but women just haven't quite got the hang of it. I'm sure that women though will say the same about us. Thing is with a penis you hardly need a map to find the right spot do you now. Men do sometimes often joke about these things though, one of my best friends had to agree with me when I would joke and he would say,

"They should do it as though they are trying to break it, almost detach it, try and rip the thing off." Trouble is that's quite a difficult thing to bring up with you latest girlfriend, so if ever asked you simply would tell them that they are doing fine. It takes them a lot longer but they get there eventually, usually with a little help from you. I mean can you imagine telling her that she was no good? There's your last chance her ever trying it for at least a month.

You find it difficult to bring up having sex with you first girlfriend and hope that soon one of your late night romps in the car will go that little bit further and you can produce that out of date condom that you have carried so proudly for the past year and slip it on and finally have sex. That usually is the way if your both virgins and its a hurried experience that you hope will soon be bettered.

So finally the waiting is over and as you realise that now is the time. Shit what's it going to be like, will I be ok; will I enjoy having sex with her? Will it last long enough so she doesn't laugh? All these thoughts are running around in your head. There is so much pressure. Eventually thank God she takes the lead and starts to take off your jeans. From there it all seems to be a blur but then your realise as your fumbling. For the first time that's all that you're really thinking about. You don't think about what you have done, it's just the fact that you have done it. We abuse the fact that there is supposed to be love and tenderness and sensual feelings evolved. Hell this is the first time and I have just had sex.

Then you finally get over the embarrassment of climbing off her and getting rid of the condom out the window and immediately ask her if she enjoyed it. They probably think typical male, even now they need their ego stroked a bit. I mean we have to know if we live up to are standards. Truth is imagine how we would feel if they said that it was crap and hurt too much, or even worse that they didn't feel very much!!!

Inevitably your first time is always rushed and quickly forgotten as neither of you know really what you should be doing but this all gets worked out in time. Then you look down at this gorgeous sweaty scrunched up beauty in the back seat of your car you realise…. Holy shit… God you've just had SEX.

The world is a happy place and nothing stops you feeling more of a MAN and you know that you are totally in love. You really need to take her home now so that you can go and tell your best mate all about it. It's a wondrous memory and one that we seem to take great pride in for the rest of our lives…we have all had those conversations…

"So come on then who was your first?"

And then we reflect into the darkest corner of our mind and remember that first time. How you felt and the Girl that we did it with. What were we doing? We should have waited. They are all of the statements that you go through your mind after the event. Yet soon realise that it was just important to have Sex with a reasonable looking girl. As long as she was normal had a big pair of tits and a pretty face that's all we basically cared about. Although I can remember that some of my friends weren't even that choosey.

Their philosophy was if they are willing then I'm going to be able. There were some monsters around. And there was always one monster that most had visited for a quick knee trembler, you would here bits of conversations and soon realise that you knew this girl now labelled as a "slag" because she had satisfied a few boys. Still everybody took the piss out of her but would have given her a go if they had the chance. Its funny how fickle we all become in those pubescent years.

"You ever shagged a fat ugly bird" my friend would often ask.

"No. Why"?

"Cos they'll let you do anything to em" he would respond simulating a shagging movement whilst clutching his groin.

Is this what we have sunk too I would ask…. hey I'm a fat git..so I cant be too choosey he would say. Then proceed to tell me of the fattest and ugliest girl he had devoured.

Reality:

Anyway back to your thoughts on your new love that had just removed your virginity for you and to whom you shall always remember for the rest of your life for doing so. More likely that you'll forget her far quicker that she'll forget you. Women are far more sensitive about loosing their virginity than men. We see it as some challenge that has been set down by our fellow men to be broken, where as the fairer sex seem to want to hang on to it till they meet the right man??? God us blokes will settle for almost anyone in the right boundaries. I mentioned that earlier.

So the relationship is bouncing along very nicely thank you and everyday you realise that you cant live without seeing this young dream and if you cant see her then your on the phone all night with her. Things in your life just couldn't be better and you know that she feels the same. You read the card that she sent you telling you how she had never felt like this before and enjoy the warm feeling that is inside your stomach. She is perfect for me and you think of your next time together. You have a nice feeling about life and feel part of the "in" crowd as you now have a girlfriend.

Then just as you are getting ready to meet her preparing for your big night out you get a phone call, and immediately you know by the tone of her "Hello" that there is something wrong….

You get a strange feeling in the pit of your guts. This is weird but also uncontrollable, now all you can do is wait for what it is she had to say…

"Look I just don't think that this is working out" She says uneasily…

Immediately you find your mind racing in circles trying to decipher the words that she just said because it sounded like she didn't think that it was working out. Now an involuntary numbness is developing in your body your not quite sure how to react, surely she cant be saying this as your meant for one another.

"What do you mean?" you eventually say in your steadiest voice.

"Look there is no easy way to say this but I don't want to see you anymore and the thing is you're a really nice person and……"

You don't really hear anymore after that, you know that she is talking to you but that strange feeling that you couldn't place just reminds you of the girl at primary school, except this time you know what it is and then find yourself firing a million questions to her, confessing your undying love for her, reminding her of the fact that you spoke about the future together and what about the holidays that you planned together. That's when she tells you that you can still be friends and hangs up with the final words,

"I am sorry."

Yeah like she means that…..!

You struggle to put the phone down knowing that once you have reality will bite you really hard and it will sink in that your glorious relationship "IS OVER". Why? What went wrong? How could she?

Then you torture yourself by feeling that you miss her already, you remember the things that you did together and that your really going to miss her, all the times that she said how much she liked you! …. What a lying bitch you would begin to think, she was just lying all of the bloody time. Why is it that men take being dumped so very hard?

These memories of our first love and heartache rarely pop into our heads until an old photo or a reminiscent conversation with an old school friend brings them back for a short time and we smile and maybe laugh out loud to ourselves.

In fact as you have just read the last few pages you have probably taken a trip down memory lane and giggled to your self about your first love and the girl that you lost your virginity with. Your thinking about something that you've probably got hidden away somewhere in the depths of your secret box. That gift or object that really meant something years ago, your also thinking about digging it out later now that you've remembered it, just for old time sake, after all that is why you kept is isn't it, so use it.

Of course there are some people who are reading this might be thinking god you soft shit!!!! They were the love em and leave em sorts who just didn't give a shit about their next date or next shag...why? ...Because they were hard and wanted everyone to know that they were men at the tender age of 16....no woman was going to break their heart...

Yet we all know that they are the loser deep down and secretly when in their own thoughts they would be pissed of and a bit gutted but never allow this to show.... they dealt with these setbacks on there own in their own time and didn't let anybody know how it effected them.

I can remember when the first real love that I had told me that she didn't think that it was going to work out, at first I was angry, then that sick feeling in my stomach returned.... and this is where you learn the emotional power that Women can have over us Men and it changes your life, it is an unexplained phenomenon, emotions and I'm not even going to try and understand the why's and the when's, that s what psychiatrists are for, so all I can do it is explain it as it happened to me.

When the late teenage years relationships get more involved you believe yourself grown up and responsible. Yet when it ends you try and deal with it sensibly.

When the phone call ended I can remember sitting there in shock, I had moved half way around the country for this cow, well that's what she is now a cow and a bitch....aargghh I hate her....oh no I don't I really love her.

After uncontrollably crying in my room for a while I began trying to gather my thoughts and then deep down inside I knew that there was only one person in the world that I could call..........MUM.

It's only at these emotional times that we learn the true meaning of being mothered. Mum always makes things better again, after trying to disguise the pain inside and trying to chat about work and how the weather is blaa blaa your Mum gently digs and asks what's wrong love, she knows instantly when there is something wrong I think that they have a sixth sense about it, and can detect the subtle changes in your voice and she already knows that something has upset you, still they continue to protect their sons feelings and say

"You seem little upset darling is everything ok?"

Inside your just about to burst with emotions yet you remain fighting the urge to let go as you don't want to look completely pathetic in front of Mum so in a stutter you try to carry on and say yes everything is fine…..then that feeling comes back again and you remember why you phoned, the numbness that you cant pinpoint it's a wave of a feeling that stirs from nowhere and ends up tugging at your stomach its like the feeling that you get just before your sick you kind of sit there and think, oh…that's a weird feeling what's all this about, and before you can register it………….splat!!!

It's too late and you have just vomited for Europe the same kind of thing happens here except instead of being sick you just let go of the waterworks and tears, spit snot the whole lot comes out all at the same time as you are trying to tell her what's wrong. She's left me Mum and from then on Mum cant really decipher what your saying and just does her best to sympathise and calm you down which slowly works and she tells you to come home…no I'm alright really, and you know that she will convince you in a minute and so you wait for the third request for you to return home and you cave in.

I then jumped in my car and drove home to mums as fast as I could. I sat in silence for a moment, being very careful to wait to be out of sight and earshot of Dad. Then as Mum sat next to me and just asked if I was ok I tired to answer but the tears start to fall again and you just let it all out again to Mum. This time it's easier as she is there to hold you and tell you its all going to be alright then hours later you begin to feel slightly better. Mum always makes things better! You feel stupid afterwards for letting go of your emotions like that and you imagine how stupid that you must have looked, but who cares as it made you feel better about it all.

You soon learn after the first time that young loves come and go and admittedly you hurt some people yourselves and you do feel bad about it for the little mourning period afterwards, which usually would last until your next night out and with your friends. Some times though you have to admit to yourself that some men are heartless and don't really care about the fact that we just slept with our girlfriend's best mate! Oopppss.

We should be racked with guilt but we don't feel that. Yet least we not forget Men that the tables to us seem to be changing and we find that more and more of us Men have been cheated on these days and I am beginning to think that things are level in the cheating stage. You can probably remember as I can that it just hardly ever happened, the bird cheated on the bloke….no she never, did she? But birds don't do that, god what a bitch! I always knew she was a wrongun.

It was a shock to the system in the Male world women just didn't do it. They were always the hurt animals. Although if we think about it, I am sure that we have all returned the favour probably more times than we would remember and care to admit too. We have all ended a relationship without thinking for one moment how it affects the other person. It is a rare thing when someone ends a relationship and genuinely cares for the other person. I mean if they cared then they wouldn't finish the relationship. I think that we have all heard the old favourite saying,

"Oh I love you but I'm just not IN love with you!!!!" I mean come on please what the hell is that all about. Where do women get this? I think that someone somewhere has told women that it's the only line that can get them out of a relationship with no problems and that the man will say oh ok well she still loves me!!

I can remember finishing a relationship with one girl and she was a little more upset that I and her leaving dig at me was to underline a couple of quotes in a little quote book that friends had given me as a present. I can't remember the author so forgive me for that but one of the quotes went pretty much like this:
"Man is the Hunter, Woman is his prey, we hunt them down and they love us for it!"

I think whoever wrote it must have had a good insight into the opposite sex, either it was a bragging Man, (Most likely say all the female readers) or a spawned woman (More like it says the male readers.) which ever I think that it paints a feminist view of the situation into the stereotypical male environment again. But these days the quote could quite have easily have started "Woman is the Hunter, Man is her prey!" I truly believe that Rudyard Kipling got it spot on when he point's out that,

"The Females of the species is more deadly than the male".

Even if you don't read poetry, never have done or never want to, then you should in your lifetime read one, when you plan to read that poem you should make it Rudyard's one. It would appear from the poem that Rudyard had been having a few problems with his women when he had sat down to pen that one. It is an eye opener and really makes you think about women in a different light. Or he met the first few feminist's who were fighting the cause, way back then when ever he wrote it.

The main point is that until you meet that real special person who really makes a difference in your life every other relationship that you have ever had was just foundations chaps. I know that it is the same for Women and that they too have to learn about affairs of the heart from being hurt, how else would we all know that we had feeling's for someone unless they hurt us? It would seem that decades ago, women had it harder than us Men and I have to admit that from what I have seen in the old black and white movies that they did get the sticky end of the stick.

However I think we have all realised Men are starting to be passed the sticky end. We have all heard about the Husband beater's and laughed...but I'm sure in a similar situation we would have just left…. why don't they? Simple…because they love them no matter how much they beat them. This is the same I'm sure for the Women who stay with the violent husband because they can see past the beatings. Strange situations I know and we all think that they are stupid for remaining yet we can only really give opinions like that when we have been in the same relationship. Who knows what really goes on?

You always need to know both sides of the story to form an opinion, but would we ever get that? I don't think so as people will always side with the person that they know or are close to. Or others outside will just side with the more believable story.

I looked upon my tragedy that follows as a possible revenge from God for the feminist movement also making me think now hang on is God a woman? Its punishment for all of the times that I had dumped someone or upset them without much care, you know where you stamp all over their heart publicly and humiliate them by dating the other girl from the group all of these thoughts enter your head as to why it has to happen to you. Sometimes I really was a heartless bastard that rarely had the guts to tell them the truth, yet how many of us have that courage. We can all say its because we didn't want to hurt their feelings, but know that its because we would rather just let it slip away than confront it and tell the truth. This does change slightly as we learn and get older though. The weaker get stronger with age and knowledge. We do learn eventually that its better in the long run to be completely honest and come clean at the very start. It saves time and further heartache later.

It can't just simply be that they don't love us or find us less attractive that just doesn't happen does it? The real question is How do you know when your in love, is she the one? Of course if I could answer that then I wouldn't be sat here telling you tales of heartbreak would I! I suppose you don't really know if you are in love until your completely immersed within it.

That is a really crap statement to make but on that day you will realise your heart feels completely different. You cant think straight, you miss the smell of her hair, her smile, her giggle, all of these things create a combination of the factors of love, for its not one thing that makes you love someone, its countless things and you find new ones everyday. A good piece of advice though is that when you find these little things each day and find yourself changing into what you think is love…. protect it, look after it, do all you can to keep it because its rare! And you will miss it when its gone oh believe me you will miss it when its gone. Women say that Men only want what they can't have. And that when they have it they don't want it any more! I'll leave you to answer that one chaps…. be honest!

Of course it does affect us all in different ways, we will all feel different about finding someone who makes us very happy in all aspects of a relationship. Although they are rare to find. So if you manage to find a person who gives you everything that you need in a relationship then sticks with it and don't mess it up.

As you fall in love things start to get even more complex and meaningful. I guess that this is the real reason for writing down what happened to me. In many relationships we do get hurt and when we are in them we truly believe that we loved that person, as we all have done. It almost becomes a fairy tale romance that expends over the rest of your life. You know that in the future your going to be together with many children, still seeing the same group of friends who are also married...imagining growing old together with your love. Looking forward to the trials through life that you will face good and bad. You enjoy life to the full and often reflect in quiet moments just how bloody lucky you really are. You're prepared for the long haul and never think or foresee any problems. There is no preparation that you take, its just all learnt on experience through the ghosts of relationship passed. You think your ready.

Yet nothing really prepares you for the time when you are really truly in REAL LOVE with somebody that you have talked and planned the rest of your lives together with. It's a trip into the unknown yet a pleasant one that you have no doubts about or hang-ups. Enjoy it as you travel through it, as it really is an enjoyable life changing experience that you may only get one chance at.

So then REAL LOVE takes these sad feelings that you once had from broken down relationships and puts them all in a different category.

Because when your in REAL LOVE and that relationship breaks down for whatever reason … … then, well speaking from experience this is what happens :

Real Love:

I was currently going through life as I'm sure we all have travelling from relationship to relationship trying to fine the one that was special. I know that we enter all of our relationships in the hope that they will turn into the special one we dream of but I had been going through a bad patch of dead end relationships and had wondered if the special soul mate that I was supposed to find actually existed at all.

It is strange to worry about this at such a young age, but I know that I wanted to just settle down and have children with someone special. I have always been a family orientated person and maybe I wanted that too much?

People say that you shouldn't wish your life away and take it as it comes to you, but I have been one of those people who get lonely and bored with life just watching TV and hoping that on the next big night out im going to meet someone of my dreams. They say that it you go out looking for love that you will not find it. It will find you they say. Others work on the old fate thing, which I have never had any belief in. Not being one to knock someone else's belief but it has never worked for me. Others say that you make your own destiny and can create your paths in life, which I suppose could have more credibility than fate in my view. I mean you can decide to do different things and try a different angle on life but in the end of the day whatever happens happens and there isn't much we can do about the way that we feel or react to things in life, we are what we are.

It's all part of the fun learning about ourselves and thinking that we are pretty well off in the great scheme of things. If we sit and think about it we are but that never makes us feel better when we think that we are hard done by. Our parents would always tell us that there are starving children in the world, people who are dying because they don't have water or simple medicine. We think about them then but it's only a quick thought and it goes away. There are not many people in the world who actually do anything about it.

If we all missed the lottery one week and gave that money to children in need then there total that week would be over 15 million just from lottery stakes. But human nature is the thought that hang on a minute that one pound could win me 15 million, so I'll play the lottery instead. Just think though if on that week we all said ok lets just miss it this once. I know that the majority of people do give to the needy but its never enough. It does help but once a year isn't going to solve their problems. So I guess when we do stand back and look at what is going on around us we are all very lucky.

So the search for happiness in life was niggling away at me and I wanted to find a relationship that was going to go somewhere and make me happy for the rest of my life. Just when I was thinking that this was something that wasn't going to happen even at my tender age of 23 but lets not forget we all think that we are older than we are and so much more grown up that we are. We learn only later in life that we still have lots to learn and will continue to learn for a very long time. One question relating to this is when do your parents stop feeling the need to govern you. We all get annoyed with them sometimes and say to others, god they still treat me like a child and yet when the tell us something we revert to that small child looking up to them. We always feel like the child and I think that we will until that dreadful day we all must face when they are not here. Me personally I would be happy to feel ruled over by my parents for a very long time as the thought of them not being here is one that I have never thought of and have no intention of even thinking about. Even putting that is writing is scary as im fighting to stop the thoughts of them not being here.

Parents are the solid foundation that we all have. Everyone's foundations handed down by parents are different which is something that is beyond our control. We are many different bits of many different people over the generations and somehow they all fit together and we are the result. Yet the world would be boring if everyone was the same thought wouldn't it.

But as I said in my search for a serious relationship started to come together slowly. I met a very special person in 1994. I had known her very distantly prior to this and hadn't really taken any notice before, I guess that at that stage in my life I was too loved up in myself I suppose and was just getting out of life what I could, I was always a happy go lucky guy and didn't always treat life with the true respect that it deserves, but then who does at the age of 23, not many of us, we just want to live fast and bugger the consequences whatever they are, booze all night drinking the most outrageous concoctions that were ever dreamed up in the bars and dance like a demented monkey truly believing that we looked great.

You could guarantee that on the way home weaving and bobbing off the walls you would find the local flea pit that was serving up anything which slightly resembled food which they probably had killed that day out the back of the shop and you would always ask him to put chilli sauce and salad on it and drool until he had wrapped it in fifteen layers of paper which you so elegantly removed and then stood swaying on the pavement outside devouring this dead carcass remembering to carefully remove and discard the chilli peppers that you had asked for. This Kebab you had just scoffed would soon to be seen again as you hurled it over the next shop front, being careful to miss the homeless person sleeping in it.

When we first got together it was a great relationship and we made each other laugh a lot which to me is the key of life, laughing is always good. We spent all the time together that we could and making love was always special, it just felt right and it was different to anything that we had ever known before. Feeling a warmth inside that hadn't been there before, yet you don't fully realise this at the time, its one of those things that slowly crept up on me. I just enjoyed our time together and didn't think much passed the immediate future, it was just nice to be in a relationship with somebody that made me happy and with somebody that quite honestly I knew really liked me a lot, to the point where she would have done anything for me and I knew that which was probably a bad thing because sometimes took advantage of that, never in a horrible way, I just knew that she would always be there no matter what, if I called her at three in the morning and asked her to come over then I knew that if she could then she would, but I never abused this or took advantage of that. Yet it does give the old ego a bit of a boost I must say.

You get a feeling of being wanted and a certain arrogance about the relationship almost knowing that you don't have to do very much except be yourself, for it is your normal self that they fell for. I know that we have all been in relationships before where we have to be slightly different and change our character to keep the relationship going, having to work at it. This is good for us to learn yet sometimes can be very demanding. I'm sure you can all recall those ex girlfriends who were very demanding in the attention department…who had to be told how much you love them all the time yet the only reason we do this is because they are probably the best looking woman that we have ever been with and want to keep her. Yet this can only last so long as love is a two way street and you realise that you too need attention and compliments every now and then.

So, we dated heavily for a while and think that I can confidently say we both liked each other a lot and I realised that this had passed the normal length of time that my usual relationship lasted and also could start to see things further down the line, this was a bit scary as I had not thought about these kind of things before in such detail or with such frequency. Even though I had been searching for it I was now a bit scared of the old commitment issue to be with this person forever!

I mean in previous relationships I was used to just thinking until the end of the week, as to when I might see the latest girlfriend for more than a few hours, things changed in years to come when you would think about holidays together…maybe and meeting the parents was always something that didn't bother me or make me think anything more about a girl, but to a girl you meeting her parents is such a big thing. It symbolises to them the beginnings to a long-term relationship. Can you imagine going home to meet Daddy's little girl. It's a dreaded day yet you know that eventually it was going to happen and you feel good about it as she wants things to move to the next level and meet the family.

Upon arrival they always stand there the welcoming committee, this usually comprises of the Mother younger sibling and the pet Labrador and of course Daddy is the missing one and always has to appear later to assume the grand entrance and command the respect that he deserves for bringing this lovely creature into the world.

He always seems to appear just as you have sat down too, so that you have to get to your feet and go through the awful masculine display of shaking hands. A display of Alpha males territory and one in which he must dominate by winning the stronger handshake. He does this cleverly by applying just that little bit more pressure than you and you can see by his forced smile and glint in his eye that you had better watch out as he is watching you. That first look says it all. It has a pleasant front but passed the first seconds you know that he is sizing you up and making his opinion of you...quickly. He is bear like and bigger than you in both size and presence. This is not what you were hoping for yet you remain respectful and cant wait to leave the room.

Those first meetings are both exciting and treacherous. Yet if you have a daughter you can probably now understand that years later what that feeling is all about. Imagine your own Baby Girl all of a sudden is going out with this young spotty teenager in front of you and he is only thinking about one thing…having sex with you daughter. It's enough to enrage any red-blooded male. Still meeting these bears over the years teaches you respect and fear of the Father. The fear is mainly down to the fact that they too were young once and know exactly what is going through your mind, SEX SEX SEX and lots of it. Yes he was there once and if you were his friend back then he would love to sit and brag about the amount of sex that he was having. But wait a minute now all bets are off as this is his princess that you are groping and fondling with at every chance you get.

I would rather meet those bears as apposed to the few Fathers that I have met who are completely hen-pecked. I feel so sorry for those who clearly jump when the wife shouts. It appears that they are almost living their life in the wrath of the wife.

This sad existence usually leads to the two of you at a later stage having bonding time in his garage while he pretends to fix the car so he can escape the dragon in the house and takes these opportunities to enforce his pretence as a man and throw insults at his wife through the garage wall and he is allowed to smoke there king in his own little kingdom master of all!

All there is for you to do is laugh and try to make him feel better. He probably knows that you have seen him for what he is but why spoil that upper hand that you have. Why crush a man when he has been crushed for twenty-five years. Why doesn't he leave her you wonder, truth is because he probably realises that to find somebody now at his age of 50 to let him have his monthly conge cal rites are non-existent. So he remains the hen-pecked Alpha Male. We could laugh at these men but then there is a tiny thought in the back of our minds that says holy shit imagine if that turns out to be me!!!!

So in my new wondrous relationship I was having different thoughts. Ones that were different and new, its sounds stupid but I started to really miss not being with her when she wasn't there and wanted her to be with me. I can remember being slightly pissed off if she hadn't called when she said she would. I was loosing control of my emotions and then I guess you could say that I didn't like these new emotions and got cold feet and wondered what I was getting into, this was a vague feeling, and it carried on for a while and I ended the relationship. That was very selfish but I couldn't control the situation so the best thing for me was to get back on control. So I ended it, how mature is that? How very Alpha Male…. Must Get Back In Control. To us men control is the most important thing. or so we would have people believe, maybe we just don't like being the one who had to make all the moves. I mean surely that's girls stuff isn't it. Some would agree but I was the one looking for a long-term heavy relationship why had I just thrown it all away. Maybe I wasn't really ready for all of that and just wanted to get out.

I think that at that time I was being forced into a situation that I wasn't ready for. it was probably my own paranoia lack of control and thoughts of what I was missing.

It always seemed to be the way that when you had a girlfriend other women would take interest in you and you had offers. Yet when you were single it's as if all the single women in the world had been removed. That I suppose is a case of the grass being greener on the other side. I mean come on chaps how many times have you peeked over the fence and thought about cutting your neighbours grass. Unfortunately sometimes you chaps jump the fence and cut the grass and the hedges and prune the bloody trees. That's what gives us the stereotypical male tarnish. Although we have all be there and done it. Even women though have done it. Its not a publicised as the men but they do it too. It's the young males dream though isn't it. The experienced older woman just using us!! How terrible of them.! (Yeah right like we were going to complain)

The cutting edge though is that you only moan when you get caught. I mean what makes men cheat on women? Some would say Women. Well that is true because he is either not in a real love situation, or very weak on will power or the best excuse it that he was pissed!!!! Yet these days there are more and more cases of the Woman having to find the excuses as to why they strayed and picked the fruit off is banana tree.

"You don't pay me any attention anymore and he treats me like a princess…"

That's the time to walk away chaps… And also the same goes for the women too. Unfortunately the mans answers is usually that she lets him have sex with her all the time!

The cliché is that the other an is only treating her like a princess because he wants to have sex with her all of the time.

Anyway after I had ended my relationship for selfish paranoia emotional reasons or whatever I had convinced myself of the thing was,I realised what a stupid Bastard that I had been and regretted my decision. This inner emotional loss stayed with me for a long time and I constantly pretended to myself that it was something else, probably just that I needed sex but was also constantly wishing that I hadn't split up with her and wished we could still be together. How many times has that happened to you? Some blokes say that its because you only crave what you cant have and that it's the anomalistic thrill of winning the prize that keeps us alive????

What's that all about? Is this a demonstration of how weak we really are? Or a true representative of the male psyche? I don't suppose that it will ever become a clear situation that we will understand.

Maybe its true in younger years to Notch up as many scalps as you can. Or maybe some of us are just still unable to sustain or fulfil that sexual desire in us. It's a search until we find the ONE to try all of them. God that sounds terrible but you'll all probably agree and the women will say

"See, I told you they were all just sexually frustrated apes."

I think that in some cases that they may be right…

What is it about the male sexual drive? Some men can go for ages without sex and not worry about getting their oats.

Then there are the others who have to jump on everything that they see in a skirt. There are obviously some psychosocial connotations that should be sorted out but hey that's why we have psychiatrists.

So eventually I had gone out with another girl which turned out to be a disastrous relationship which was one of constant comparisons that I had, thinking that well she is different in this way to her and that way to her, I had to finish that relationship and contact the ex girlfriend as I just couldn't get her out of my head. It took me a while to pluck up enough courage and eventually contact her!

So I did and luckily for me she was really happy to hear from me, which I could tell from her voice wasn't just a put on and asked if I could meet her, to my delight she said yes and I could hardly wait until the weekend to go and see her.

This is where you remember all of the good points of a relationship that you have previously been in, the good feelings of being with someone who actually liked you oh and yes the sex and the sex and the sex. Talking of Sex this then puts an immediate question inside your thought process, wondering, will we have sex?

I mean anyone who may be reading this who at some stage got back with an ex girlfriend will understand these thoughts and I'm sure that we all wondered the same thing, how long will it be before we have sex again. I mean don't forget the sex was always great. Will she let you stay or will you be heading home on that late train or bus? These are not all of the points that you think about, you do think I wonder if she is still the same looking, still as pretty, the same weight? God imagine if she has put on a couple of stone!!!!! I mean you can hardly ask her that over the phone can you, yet you have these small thoughts on the way to see her but you convince yourself that your being a bit paranoid and that your sure she is everything that she was.

When I got there and looked at her I knew how much I was glad to see she hadn't put on two stone and still looked incredible and understood immediately that I still liked her and it was as if everything was the same as if we never were apart. After a few drinks in the pub to get over the initial meeting the nerves soon disappeared we were holding hands and sharing the odd cuddle, and then the little jokes would come from her about me dumping her which I had to confess how stupid that I was and hope that she would consider possibly going out with me again, (humble pie is so very bitter yet you know that it is a small price to pay) she did and again it was wonderful, travelling down to see her and her travelling up to see me. It began to feel that we had never been apart and I wished more and more that we hadn't of been, but hey that's behind us now and were back on track and I was more than happy again. Each time we met things just got better and romance soon bloomed again.

After a few months of travelling to see each other we took jobs near eachother and moved in to a little flat in London. Now living with someone 24 hours a day was a new concept for me but I felt ready to give it ago. It is a difficult decision to make and a tough one to call. How do you know that you wouldn't hate it? Start fighting? The answer is simple.... you don't know if it is going to work, but judged on the time that you have spent together and the way that you feel about each other you just have to give it a take a chance and give it a go. I began to learn that I worry about things too much that could possibly happen. This is a stupid thing to do, but I can't help it.

Everything seemed to be better that I had ever known in a relationship or to be honest thought that it could be. I loved my Job had a great home life and really felt happy. This continued for the next few months and I just loved life.

Then out of the blue for some reason and to this day I don't know why I began to feel uneasy again with the relationship. I kept quiet at first and tried to just get through this feeling whatever it was. It wouldn't go away though, surely I couldn't do this again to her not twice. I knew that I liked her and cared for her a great deal because I felt terrible about the thought of leaving her and began to think of how much she would hate me for doing this to her again if I broke it off. I missed my friends and family and the comfort of familiar surroundings that I had at home. I fought at these feelings for a little while and decided that I just wasn't happy for whatever those reasons were and decided to tell her.

I knew that this wasn't going to be an easy task and thought about what I would say and tried to anticipate what she would have to say in return. You convince yourself that she will be fine and then run through small thoughts that maybe she feels the same way and just doesn't know how to say it to you, wouldn't that be a turn up for the books. What if you left it for a little while longer she might say it first and then that would make it easier. You could pretend to be upset and pissed off. But wait what if you did that and she then changed her mind because she thought that you didn't care but now she could see that you did, Jesus how the hell would you back up out of that one.

So I knew that I had made the right decision and had to tell her.

We had planned a holiday and had to go away after my news that we should break up. This admittedly was a strange decision to make going on holiday with a girlfriend that you intended to split up with upon your return. And thinking about it even stranger that she wanted to still go. I suppose if you analyse it she may have done it in the hope that things on holiday might change between us. I suppose in some way that was at the back of my mind too. It was kind of a last quest into the depths of what a relationship is all about and to see if things could change in a relaxed environment away from everything. We did have a good time and enjoyed our week away, but I didn't find what I was looking for and when we returned home we did split up again. I took her to her Fathers house with my car full of all her belongings and remembered driving away feeling relieved but also a little sad.

Unfortunately this relief was only short lived.

I thought the best thing was to try and forget about what had happened and put it to the back of my head. Its over so move on…get on with your life. So the normal Friday and Saturday nights began of sheer alcohol abuse and the search for my queen began again (Although generally all I seemed to find lurking about were the ugly sisters!!!)

During this time I regained contact with an old girlfriend from when I lived in Dubai. I met this girl when I first moved there and was caught up in a relationship with her when I met my now ex-girlfriend. This got a little messy, as when I met my ex to be she was in a relationship and so was i. But people keep saying that the path of true love never ran smoothly. Jesus they weren't kidding. It remained the typical love triangle for a while where I was sort of still seeing the girl and my ex had been kicked out of her boyfriends flat and turned up on my doorstep at three in the morning and asked if she could stay.

Shit....now what am I going to do! I supposed to be seeing someone and now the girl I was having an affair with has moved into my apartment. What should I do??? The cowardly thing of course and continually lied. Eventually lies caught up with me as they always do and was deep in the shit. The girl I was seeing disposed of me as the cheating liar I was and now ex had to leave the country and go home. This was because her ex had discovered the truth about us and phoned her employer and got her sacked. He told them about our affair and of course in Dubai you have to live by their rules and they frown upon such behaviour so they declined to renew her contract. Anyway that kind of ended both relationships for the time.

But when my ex returned home I managed after some time to talk to the girl in Dubai and began to have the odd date and slowly reformed a relationship.

We chatted a few times and realised there was still a spark there and arranged to meet in Paris as she would be there in a few days. It was a big adventure to me and I was nervous about meeting her and the inevitable questions about what I had been doing. To tell the truth would really piss her off as I had been living and having a relationship with the very person that split us up. I decided that if that came up to come clean and tell the truth for once in my life. One of my best friends taught me a long time ago to always tell the truth. If you always tell the truth then you will never get caught out in your own web of lies. This makes complete sense but we all have to start telling the truth somewhere so I took his advice and thought that I would be ok as the truth usually ends up being ok.

Christ what a big mistake that turned out to be….

I told her after a lovely night of dinner and drinks in Paris. She asked me so I told her what had been happening to me. I told her everything about my ex girlfriend and how she was the girl that I had been seeing in Dubai.

She ignored me for the net couple of hours and wouldn't speak to me. It's not easy having a one-way conversation and falling over your past. I mean you can only apologise so much cant you?

Eventually I managed to sort it out and she began to speak to me. There were lots of awkward questions and the past was all dragged up and I found it difficult to tell the truth as it kept dropping me further an further in the shit, but I stuck with it and could here my friends words in my head. "Just tell the truth and it will all be ok"

Eventually the questions stopped and we were able to patch over the difficult conversations and begin to talk about us.

After our Paris encounter we started to meet regularly as she flew back and forth to the London. A few months later whilst taking a weeks holiday over here together we got engaged!!!!!

Now you may be surprised at this as it was my second engagement but I had the thought, liked her a lot, asked her to get engaged to me and she said yes…bought the ring and it was done.

Oh my God…. what had I done.

Talk about having impulsive moments. How could I have done this?

Making important decisions wasn't something that I had a lot of experience in and so they don't seem such a big deal. I don't think that at such a young age we really understand the full consequences of decisions and actions that we end up taking, especially in a highly emotional circumstance. Why did I take this thing so lightly? Because I didn't know any different. I like the way that people react when they are in love and enjoy making people happy and excited but be careful when you make decisions in a highly emotional state.

Everything just seemed to happen and I was certainly swept along with it all. The excitement the happiness and the thought of life together and married. This was what I wanted right? I meant I did think this all through didn't I?

I remember telling my parents on the telephone. My Dad bless him offered congratulations straight away and seemed very happy that I was happy, my Mum was very happy for me to. We had the meals and celebrations with both families and everyone was genuinely happy that we had done this. People were also shocked and all probably said things behind our backs about how quick it was and some had never even heard mention of her or me.

The engagement was official now and everyone had given us his or her good wishes. Some no doubt would have said it wouldn't last! But hey what did they know?

Quite a lot it turned out as it was short lived and kind off fizzled out after a month or so. To this day I don't know why I did it of fizzled out so quickly. I suppose that there is the rebound situation, I just think that I took it a bit far. Sorry just couldn't get me out of this one. I have no real substantial explanation of the whole thing. I thought that I loved her, and im sure at the time that I did yet she was someone that I could love for the rest of my life? Could she really be the one? But it felt inside that she wasn't. There was just something there all of a sudden that made me stop and question my true feelings for her and our relationship.

I didn't know what it was yet knew it wasn't going away. Maybe should have waited a while before moving so quickly into an engagement. What a complete ass I was. I took the easy way out and let the small heated discussions turn into more and more heated arguments until she would blow her stack and slam the phone down. Pretty shitty I know but I was in a corner and should have told the truth but chickened out again. The inevitable happened and the relationship just fell apart bit by bit until it was obvious to both of us that it was over. I don't think that we ever sat there and said "ok look this is going nowhere and both of us know its over, so lets end on a sensible note and get on with our lives" no that would be far too easy and adult.

I seemed over the years to develop a pattern of going out with ex girlfriends most of the time. I think that this was because I felt far more comfortable with someone that I already knew and had a connection with. It's also easier to go out with an ex if I'm honest. You know their routine and they know yours. Maybe I'm just a creature of habit and I don't like too much change?

So here I was single again and I had the thoughts that maybe I was meant to be a bloody monk!!!

What will happen next?

I decided to just be single and free for a while! What is it they say?

"To try and find myself…" what crap that is…. it's just a matter of thinking and making decisions. Thought they have to be practical ones from now on!!!

After "finding myself" I began to review what had been happening to me over the past few years. Reviewing the situation for all I had done! These thoughts led me back to the girl from Dubai that I had been with and left then been with and left again. I know what your probably saying, no you cant do it. Yet there were the thoughts of her there in my head and they wouldn't go away. Why was I so fucked up in the head about relationships? Did God pick me out of a line up and decide that I was to be confused by women all of my life. It certainly seemed that way back then. Surely I should just leave the past well alone and try to get something else out of life.

Maybe we are supposed to be together. I certainly still had feelings for her. God do I dare contact her? Fuck I mean what would she say about the engagement!!!! I realised that I missed her and over the next few weeks knew that I hated not being with her yet for some reason kept running from her. Eventually it had got to the point where I had to contact her. This was a brave move and I thought that she would just tell me once and for all to just FUCKOFF. That put me off the call for a while but she was still there and I had to know if she felt the same as me. So I made the call and she did so we agreed to meet.

For whatever reason I now knew that this Woman was the first ever to control my heart strings and I had never had such feelings in a relationship before where I felt more at ease and happy with her, it had just taken me a long time to come to this conclusion but I now knew after missing her for all of the times that we had been apart that I think that I was in "REAL LOVE" for the very first time in my life and that I didn't want to risk being stupid anymore. I knew that there was a feeling inside that I had for her that was very strong unlike others that I had ever had towards a woman. This was weird and I knew deep down that I had been completely stupid and should have made this decision a long time ago. Look at all of the time that I had wasted where we could have been together.

Never look back people say, but that's only because they have done it and know what crap it brings. It's human nature to look back and reflect on what mistakes we made. You over analyse and think that you could have done this or that but why? Its far too late now as it's in the past so don't beat yourself up about it and move on with you life.

The Big Step:

After meeting up again and discussing what I had been doing over the past six months and the disastrous decisions that I had made in my life we decided to give our relationship another go.

As we talked I realised that I missed her more than I thought but knew that I had to go slowly this time and do things right. I mean would she want me again after what I had put her through?

I didn't think that she would and might just want to stay friends. But we all know exactly what that means.

Things again fell right back into place as before and I soon began to realise that for possibly the first time in my life that I was in REAL LOVE and I began to feel really relaxed in the relationship and then let life go on.

She still lived in her own environment whilst we made sure that this time I wasn't going to fuck up her life again. It was quickly apparent to her that this time I was showing more than before and I was serious about us this time. We discussed more permanent arrangements after a few months of living apart and then moved to the same town and lived in a small flat. She got a job in the same town and was happy. We wouldn't bring up the past, as it was probably best not to do that. Every now and then she would tell me bits about how I had really really hurt her and I felt a complete bastard. All I could know was get on with the present and try to show her just how committed to her I was.

It was wonderful; the normal evenings out down the pub got exchanged for nights in watching a video curled up together with the fire burning and a glass or two of wine. Its weird how for years you love to be out in the thick of the hustle and bustle of a Friday night with all of your mates, leering at the women, drinking your own weight in beer and having that camaraderie of the old friends of years, but all of a sudden in your mid to late twenties you find your first real live in love and you stay in. You find a new way of life that you didn't know existed.

Your close friends on the rare occasions would comment on how they hadn't seen you out lately, oh you must be in love they would tease…. yes I would admit its great. Then you tend to find that more and more of the socialising that you do is with other couples, meals out dinner parties, that sort of thing, and I really began to enjoy everything, even shopping together was fun, and always telling her that I loved her, not just because she might have wanted to hear it, but because I really felt it.

I used to love special occasions because then its easy to express your love for a partner through thoughtful gifts and special emotional moments, where you really make love to eachother, it is no longer just SEX as a very pleasant pass time it becomes very special and you feel so close to this person and know that you never want to change the way that they make you feel whilst making love and that you truly believe that you never want to have sex with anybody else for the rest of your life, even when they are grey and old you know that you will still love this person so very deeply, and you also get the same feelings back from them and can see it in their eyes….it really is a very special feeling one that can only be seen and felt yet could not be described anywhere near to the true feelings that you see and feel from this person.

Eyes can say so much, people say that they can look at your soul if lovers gaze at each other, now many of you reading this will think out loud, What a load of Bollocks! Yet you know that you have done that, looked deep into someone's eyes and told them you loved them. You may have done it once or twice to get them to allow you out to watch the match without them being pissed off on your return, and you probably have abused that line once or twice more, yet at least once you have looked deep into those eyes of your partner and really felt it. It probably scared the shit out of you but you felt it. If you haven't yet don't worry you will one day trust me everyone finds at least one love in their life.

Some people seem to run away from these feelings inside and know full well what they mean. Why is it so many men have hidden these away deep down and tried to pretend that they are not there. They soon remember them when they have done something wrong and upset their partner. I think that it is down to the fact that on the whole women are just far more romantic than us men. They have always been able to express their feelings better than men. Men just think that a bunch of flowers a good meal, wine and sex is the answer to everything. There are men out there ladies who are sensitive and show there love all of the time. Getting in touch with the female side they call it.

How did I know that this was right and true love? I felt it inside and knew that I wanted to be with her and felt the need to commit to her all that I was and would be for the rest of my life. Now that is a very important decision and not one to be taken lightly. It doesn't happen overnight, it builds up over a long period of time until you find the feelings that you have, good and bad help you understand it doesn't get any better than this. To miss someone for the hours that you don't spend together gives you a feeling of fulfilment in a relationship. We have all had the honeymoon period of a relationship when we feel this way but slowly that diminishes and you're both left wondering what is next after this.

Marriage.

I had planned the proposal in my head over and over again and had decided to ask her on my Birthday. We had planned to be at her Parents house over the Christmas period and so I spoke with her Mother and Stepfather about it and they were all excited about the new turn in our relationship.

Now all that was left was for me to ask her.

Shit what happens if she said no though? Oh god I hadn't thought about that. I did have a good feeling about this though and hoped that she would say yes when I asked her. So I decided to put it out of my mind the possibility that she would say no and if she did then at least I would know she didn't feel that same way as me.

Of course with all of this going on in my head I had a tiny thought that she might say no, so I had a plan that would let me know how she would feel about an engagement. For Christmas I bought her a dress ring, wrapped it up and when we had exchanged all of our presents I said that I remembered that I had one more present for her. She looked puzzled and I offered the tiny gift wrapped box and look at her face. She frantically ripped the paper of then paused looking excited and opened the box slowly. Her eyes were on stalks as she giggled and eventually opened the box. Her reaction to me said it all when she realised that it was only a dress ring and tried to pretend that she was happy and loved it. I knew then that she too felt the way that I did and wanted to get married. Maybe we are just two old romantics at heart.

So I bought the ring and fought like hell inside to keep it secret from her. I am usually terrible with secrets and end up spoiling the moment by blurting whatever it is out before I should. Yet this time I was doing well and kept my excitement under control.

We exchanged our gifts on Christmas day and then made our way up to her parent's house.

As we finished our evening meal at her parents on Christmas day I had noticed that her Mother had set up a tray of glasses filled with Champagne to have with our pudding to celebrate Christmas. With this she winked at me…

Now I was slightly confused because it wasn't my Birthday so I'm stood there thinking this is odd, drinking champagne with pudding but hey what the hell. Then I realised everyone looking at me and smiling and winking. My Wife to be though didn't know it, yet it was obvious with them all stood there grinning like Cheshire cats and she went into the other room.

"What are you lot all staring at me for...I asked with a smile..."

They looked pleased with themselves and said

"Oh as if you didn't know!!!"

"Know what?" Now I was puzzled...

"Have you got it then?" her Mum asked

"Got what?" I replied.

"Oh you are always such a joker.... the ring silly?"

"Why would I its not my Birthday"...This comment left stunned silence in the room and all eyes were on me you could of heard a pin drop. It was as if someone had pushed pause on a video. I was still very confused which was giving me a headache because we were also all a bit pissed from the dinner drinks....

"Oh God.. But I thought we were going to do it today!!" Said her Mum...

Then everyone was looking at me expectantly...waiting for my comment...

"But..Oh alright then...I'll get the ring its in the car!" with that everyone was smiling and excited again.

So I ran out to the car and fumbled around in the boot where I had hidden the ring. I was getting soaked because it was pissing down and the alcohol that I had consumed was making it difficult for me to find it never mind standing still. Eventually I found the box and came back in through the back door. My girlfriend was stood there and asked me what was going on.

"What have you been doing I was looking for you" but before I could think of an excuse she pulled me into the other room where everyone was waiting to toast in Christmas.

With video cameras everywhere and all the family stood there the Dad said a few words to toast family and friends whishing them all a Happy Christmas, then he turned to me and said,

"Just one more thing. I think that someone else has something to say"…

With that the room went drastically silent and everybody turned to look at me.

Christ I was so nervous and so very pissed… I hope that this was going to come out right.

"Why is everyone looking at you? What's going on here what's happening….

She turned to look at me with the biggest smile on her face, expectantly like children have waiting for their Christmas presents almost as if she knew but wasn't sure what was about to happen.

I can remember looking at her stood there smiling and so excited. I felt nervous but also happy that I was able to make her feel like this. With that I knew before I had asked her that she was going to say yes.

I really to this day can't remember how I started off speaking as the Alcohol made it a bit blurry. I think that I had told everyone that it was nice to see them and glad that they were here with us to share this special occasion. I was looking at my Girlfriend who was transfixed on me as if I was about to do something still with this expectant look on her face and huge smile...

With that I held her hand and dropped to one knee...with this she couldn't stop smiling and was bouncing up and down giggling with excitement and not be able to stand still, and I presented the ring and proposed.

The tears that she cried told me her answer and she just kept holding the ring and looking down at it. Suddenly we were surrounded by the family all hugging us and offering congratulations to us. Even though people were weaving in and out all we did was stare at each other through the commotion as if there wasn't anyone there.

So over the next few months we enjoyed the new status of our relationship and enjoyed being with each other even more. It was a different level in the relationship that made both of us very happy. Slowly we realised that we had to plan the wedding and started to look into all of the things that needed to be done. We met with the vicar of the local area and fixed everything with the Church. We are not strong believers in the religious side of marriage and got married at the Church in her parental home village, purely because it was old and picturesque. Arranging a wedding we learnt was harder that it sounds. You have to keep everybody happy and end up having to please so many people. Sometimes you believe that it's a day for others and not you. Hosting it in the right place, inviting the right people and of course paying for it.

We didn't think that there was much point in hanging around so planned it for the following June. Everyone was getting very excited about the big day and it seemed to be on top of us before we knew it. There were lots of arguments and disagreements along the way, which all seemed to be with her family mainly the mother but we got there in the end. So everything was arranged in time and we had the reception at her parent's house just down the road from the church.

It was a wonderful day even though it rained it didn't spoil it and lots of both families were there to enjoy it.

The comedy point of the day that everyone remembers it for happened to involve one of my oldest and best friends. My mother was entertaining some of the children and running around with them playing football when the ball was kicked into the small orchard.

My mother went to retrieve the ball but found she stumbled across something else in the long grass. There was my best friend in a rather precarious position with his girlfriend having sex in the safety of the long grass, or so they thought.

Needless to say my Mother appeared without the ball trying to shield both her embarrassment and the children from the activities currently occurring within the orchard!!!

The same two culprits were also caught later in the downstairs toilet creating quite a queue outside. "Well at least he came out relieved" said my uncle with a wink and a smile…

On that day in June though I was the happiest man in the world and nobody was ever going to take that away from me. There is nothing to top that feeling, LOVE, sometimes we dismiss it, other times we say it because it needs to be said and we know that she likes to hear it, but rarely for a MAN we really do mean it when we say it.

It's easier for some more than others to say but we all have our moments and I'm sure that we and our loved ones both know when they are. I think that more often that not people take their love and happiness for granted. We only can really appreciate it when we haven't got it.

That may sound a little cynical but I do believe that we are all guilty of taking for granted our love. We just assume that it is going to be there for all eternity and pay no attention to potential real problems. Truth is though that marriage is about learning to compromise with each other and our little idiosyncrasies, which is why the world of love is a continual learning ground.

This most of the time it is a wonderful place to be, as you are continually finding out new things about each other and learning to love or hate them. This is the challenge that comes with loving somebody. The real challenge is finding the correct soul mate that thinks like you and reacts like you to all of the problems that we encounter along the way. I truly believed that in my wife I had met my soul mate and was extremely happy to learn all about her. I suppose that to truly know someone is to love them, as they say, however I don't think that you ever truly know your partner completely. There will always be something that they do which takes you completely unawares.

As our married life continues through its path everything seemed to just get better. It is weird how when you sit back and think of it and the changes that you go through yourself. You find yourself changing without noticing at first. This is usually because of circumstances that happen when with your loved one. You're aggression, your humour, and your drive in life all changes when you have to consider another person. It's as if half your time you become one person and have to handle things as you and your partner would and this happens naturally over time

My wife and I were growing closer all of the time and enjoying life as it is supposed to be enjoyed. We had talked before about having children and both agreed that it was something in the near future that both of us really wanted. Even before we were married we would have make believe conversations about what we would call our children and the fact that we would like three or four. Now that we had grown closer and secured the rest of our life together practically we discussed the children element of our future.

We both agreed that we wanted to try for children. Was it too soon we thought? We didn't want to rush it yet after talking it over for a while we realised that it was something that we both wanted to do. We had waited until we both felt that we were with the right person. So sod what anyone else thought it's up to us and we were ready. Truth is you learn that no matter how many classes you go to or how many people that you talk to about children there is nothing to prepare you for what happens. You see there is no particular textbook baby. They are all different and will be as they are. Some people have it lucky and have a child that goes to sleep all the time, never cries and is a good as gold. It was exciting but scary too.

Yet that was all to look forward in the future I mean for starters my wife was not pregnant yet. Then the simplest thing about the human race makes you stop and think about the possibility of not being able to have children?

What if the fundamental thing that we were put on this planet for we couldn't do? God what if it was I who was the problem. We discussed this and my wife had told me not to be so silly an think about those things. Yet that made it worse as I kept thinking about it then.

"We will just think about that later if it happens"

This is a worry that I imagine all couples go through who plan to have children. This is something that you don't really need at this special time of trying to conceive a child. It puts unnecessary pressure on both of you, probably more so for the man as his performance could be hampered by the constant thought that this isn't going to work...

It does put the whole wonderful ceremony of having sex into a new ballpark. Sometimes they say that you can want a baby too much and try to hard. But the trying is the fun part. Constant sex as many times as you can. I mean guys for the first time in your life you can have what you have always dreamed off. Constant SEX whenever and wherever you can give it to each other, and not having to worry about her being pregnant, because that's what your aiming for.

Your wife seems to go into overdrive as she now needs to get pregnant more than anything in the world, but sometimes only when you suddenly think about what you are actually trying to do it does hamper it for us males. We know that it's the biggest change in our lives and that we both want it more than anything in the whole world…God talk about pressure.

I remember that the first time that we had tried for a baby we were not successful. Then you really start to worry. It was bad enough before and not the pressure was getting to me. You are slightly stressed thinking that maybe its you and that your sperm are non-swimmers or you may be "shooting Blanks" as the horrible phrase goes. This is the ultimate downside to trying for kids. Then when you have to discuss it with your partner, that your worried you have to also look at the possibility that it's your wife and not you.

"OF course it could be you also" you sympathetically say..

"Oh great thanks, try and pass on the blame to me now that you may be shooting blanks"…. This usually ends up in a n argument.

It's a tough time and you both try and relax and remind each other that it's the first time that you tried and before we start to get worried we should at least give it a few more attempts.

So you try and put this to the back of your mind, but it seems to creep to the front of your thoughts just at the point of having sex. This does spoil the occasion and you have many failed attempts. The best thing to do when this happens is to try and laugh it off and have a very understanding partner who will tell you that its just the pressure your putting yourself under and to try and relax. This slowly works and eventually I was able to put those impotent thoughts to the back of my mind and enjoy the experience of twenty-four hours a day availability of SEX!!!

On this second attempt my wife was late starting her period and was very excited. But we agreed to let nature take its course and see what happened as it had only been a few days.

"But I'm never late" she said,

"Look don't jinx it, lets just leave it a while".

After two weeks my wife could wait no longer. Having promising each other that we would let nature take its course I had returned form to the house early one Saturday after going out shopping to see my wife peering through the slightly open front door beckoning me into the house quickly. Slightly puzzled by her excitement this early on a Saturday morning I ran into the house. She was stood there wearing nothing but a towel with a big smile on her face.

I then noticed the little white stick in her hand but was a bit slow in realising what the significance was between her smiling and the white stick.

"Its positive" she blurted out with joy and flung her arms around me. With a quick hug she retreated slightly and thrust the little white stick at me for me to see the two little blue lines.

A whole new wave of excitement hit me. My god we were going to have a baby. This happiness never left me. For days I can remember not being able to believe that we were going to have a baby. Nothing seemed different. You kind of imagine an immediate change to things but there wasn't. Everyone became really excited when they heard the news and all passed their good wishes yet life went on as normal. Then again looking back I suppose it would for a while because there is no immediate change. In fact for us men there is no change. After all we have done our bit according to nature now all we could so is be supportive and wait.

Men have the easiest part in all of this we know. And I think that we would all admit that were fine with that and wouldn't change place at all. During the pregnancy there was very little change in our routine. At least for me there wasn't any change in terms of my physical state. I know that my wife was changing though very slowly. We had all of the standard tests, which are very difficult on a couple all with horrible discussions of what could go wrong. You then have a new worry that something will go wrong. Its weird that with such a joyous occasion is slightly marred by the thoughts that so very much can go wrong. These points are bought to your attention continuously and it makes you sometimes go out of your mind with worry.

You then realise that it is ten times worse for your partner as they are the one going through all of these hormonal changes and having to deal with the awful possibilities on top of that. However the hospitals are wonderful and keep checks on you all of the way through. I can remember going to one of the scans where you can see your little baby really taking shape on the screen. This makes you thank God for what he had given you and you realise what a wonderful thing you have both done. As you look at the screen you realise that the little baby shape is part of you and your partner. Almost like cutting you both in half and sticking it together.

Then the nurse asked if we wanted to know what the sex was. Now my wife and I had discussed this with the midwife who had told us that as far as she was concerned with all her years of experience that it was a boy, no doubt about it. How the hell she knew this was unbeknown to my wife and I but we had accepted her words and had set our selves up to the fact that we already knew the sex, so agreed to let the nurse tell us and confirm what we already knew.

"If you look carefully at the screen here where I'm pointing you can see three little lines. Those three lines confirm to me that you are going to have a little girl" then she smiled at us both after telling us the news."

"Are you sure?" we asked in succession, it's just that we were told it was a boy.

"No its not a boy" The nurse looked at us both with a puzzled expression,

"If you look here at the screen you can see the three lines, this is how I know that it's definitely a girl."

This took us slightly by shock, as we were sure that it was going to be a boy. After getting over the shock of the fact that it was going to be a girl and now coming to terms with this news we were able to now concentrate on the next five months to prepare for the arrival of our baby girl.

We chose a name very soon and then bump had a name, which made it feel more real. Now it was just a question of waiting for the big day. It was like waiting for all of your Christmas's and Birthday's to come at once. I was so excited and the time couldn't pass quick enough for me so that I could sit there and finally see my baby girl.

After a long pregnancy where I felt completely useless, it was an emotionally testing time, for the both of us where I couldn't seem to ever comfort my wife through any difficult situation though try as hard as I did. She may say that I had done it all wrong and didn't do enough of this or enough of that but I was new to this and I did everything that I thought I should. It was alien to both of us and it was very tough, but with the joy that you know is waiting for you at the end you manage to get passed it

We had talked about the changes that she was going through yet dismissed them saying that these would all go away after the birth. She had changed a lot during the pregnancy and towards the end it was very noticeable to lots of people. But its bound to happen. So all you can do is keep counting down the days and waiting for the arrival.

My wife was now passed her delivery date by nearly two weeks so they were going to educe her. We went to the hospital both nervous and excited about the biggest thing that had ever happened to us in our lives. They gave my wife a drug, which helps bring on the birth, and sent us back home to just sit and wait.

As you can imagine that was pretty nailbitting stuff just sitting and waiting for it to start. Most of this time you sit and watch TV trying to take your mind off it. My wife was getting more and more stressed with the waiting and all I could do was sit and listen offering support. Just as we had convinced ourselves that it was probably going to go on through the night it started, so into the hospital we went to sit and wait some more but at least, you knew that it was now imminent.

My wife had decided to have an epidural, which is a drug that is given intravenously via a line, which is put in through the gaps in the spine. Now as us men can only imagine how painful that could be and watching the doctor putting the needle in to her spine certainly made my eyes water and as its not exactly a small one.

Now having a long needle pushed in between your spine is bad enough but the complete asshole of a doctor who came in to do this almost got taken to A&E himslef. He tried about six times to get the line in but couldn't get it right. Each time taking out the needle again and trying to insert it in a new hole. By this time my wife was in sever pain, curled up in to a ball shape as best she could whilst this incompetent wanker was playing darts with her lower back. In the end I had to tell him to fuckoff in so many words and both my wife and I demanded that someone who knew what they were doing performed this task. Childbirth is a traumatic experience enough for your partner and now with the added stress of the asshole my wife was getting very upset. The main worry also is that you can damage the spinal cord if you don't get this procedure correct.

Shortly after our little outburst another Doctor was called for and within minutes entered the room. Immediately he took full control of the situation and the first challenge he had was to calm everybody down, most importantly my wife. Well I was impressed with him as he did that instantly. Hat off to him he was very good and successful and he easily inserted the line on the first attempt and was gone in a few minutes.

Later on whilst we sat and waited my parents came to check on us and make sure they could do all they could. They did that just by being there as I find they always are. All throughout my life they have been like that and I never take it for granted. They are the most wonderful parents and I love them dearly for that. They give me that marvellous knowledge that if I need them then it only takes a phone call and I know that wherever I would be even if it were half way around the world they would move heaven and Earth to get there. In that I am extremely lucky and thank them for that endlessly. I did feel slightly guilty as nobody from my wife's family was there and I knew that it bothered her even though she tried to hide it.

Her mother had even gone on holiday at the exact time when the baby was due so she didn't have to be around.

"Oh she won't want me getting in the way" she said and went.

Now I would have thought common sense would have told a mother that the single most important time in her daughters life would be this one. My wife was really upset by this but said that if her mother didn't realise this then she wasn't going to point this out.

When other people don't get on or are not close to their parents I just find it hard to believe. Again this is probably where I have been extremely lucky to have such a strong relationship with mine. It does make me feel lucky but also sad for the people who don't have a close bond with their family. It usually isn't his or her fault and to blame anyone is difficult. I just can't imagine how alone they must feel sometime.

After my parents had given us there support and left my wife told me that her waters had broken.

Holy shit.........this is it?

Through the next hours I just had to sit there and watch my wife go through the toughest task in her life and we were both scared beyond belief. You just have to hope and pray that everything goes ok without any problems. Eventually she began to dilate but not satisfactorily for the Doctor. They then started to talk about a caesarean. Jesus that scared the shit out of my wife and I and we began to worry beyond belief. Horrible thoughts start to rush through your mind about them both you think of all the horror stories that occur during this operation and the minute chance that they might die.

I was trying to remain calm on the outside to be strong for my wife but inside I was in a terrible state. My wife begged me to stop them from performing a caesarean.

"Don't let them" is all she kept saying. All I could do now was pray that they would both be ok, don't let them die is all I could think. I felt like crying for them. My wife was they're looking terrified and I felt so useless there was nothing that I could do. I told the Doctor that we didn't want a caesarean and they assured me that if possible they would rather not do that but had to consider the possibility to ensure both mother and baby were ok. You go into a blind panic because of the worry for your wife and baby and then the worry that they might have to take them away into a theatre and operate to cut the baby out. Fucking hell now that was a worry. I felt so fucking useless, why didn't I know more about this sort of stuff. But all I could do was leave it up to the people who were specialist in this. All that I could do was just hope and pray that they would both be ok!

Luckily during the next hour or so my wife began to dilate to a degree where they were happy to continue on with natural childbirth. Eventually the time was here and everything seemed to reach the point of climax. I was only able to stand there and hold her hand and watch. Time seemed to stand still as I watched my wife going through unimaginable pain.

There are few things in the world that will make you feel completely useless, this was one of those things. I wished that I could do something that was of more help, but they said that holding my wife's hand and being there was all that I could do. They warn you of these feelings in the anti natal clinic and try to tell you in the nicest way that we had done our part, also know as the "Easy Part"

Still if that wasn't enough thing's decided to get a little worse for us.

Then the Doctor told her to stop pushing, as there was something wrong. Oh fucking hell that is not what you want to here. She said that she was going to have to use forceps to extract the baby. Now I imagined forceps as little implements you might turn over a bar b q sausage. Well Fuck me. When she turned around with what I thought was a pair of very long garden shears I could have cried for my wife. They are absolutely huge. The Doctor inserted one then the other linked them together and began to lever them upwards. This little Doctor was on the edge of her seat and pulling with all her mite. What the fuck are you doing….your going to pull her inside out I thought.

"For God sake isn't that going to hurt her and the baby?" I screamed.

"Please sir don't worry its ok" the nurse assured me.

I couldn't believe what I was seeing. It must have been horrendous for my wife. Quickly the doctor stopped and realised why this wasn't working. The cord was wrapped around the babies' neck. Quick as a flash she cut it and the baby flew out. I had planned to cut the cord and was waiting for my signal but had to forget that now as there were problems.

To this day that vision remains in my head. My baby girl came out. It is difficult to describe in words and the only real way to understand is to see it for yourself. They whisked our daughter away and two nurses gathered around her on this little bed.

"What's going on? Is she ok? Will somebody tell us if she is ok".

All we could see was the back of the two nurses and couldn't hear the baby. There was no noise from her.

"Jesus Christ what is going on will somebody please tell us!"

My wife was pleading with me.

"Is she ok, what's wrong? Something's wrong isn't it? Tell me what is it".

"It'll be ok I'm sure"

"What are they doing? Why isn't she crying? What's happening?"

The next few minutes seemed to drag on through and eternity.

Please God let her be ok. I was completely numb was she ok or. ...Jesus the alternative wasn't worth contemplating!

I then saw a nurse lifting up her arm and dropping it, then a leg. It was as if she was lifeless as the arm and leg just fell back down with no resistance. Oh fuck please no...what is happening here.

The other nurse then gave her an injection in her heel. Then they waited a while and the whole room was silent and everybody was looking in their direction.

Then the eternal silence of the room was broken by the sweetest sound I have ever heard in the world. She screamed. I felt as though someone had lifted an elephant of my chest. My wife an I kissed and hugged blubbering to each other that she was ok. Then they bought her over to us.

Talk about melt away. I was hooked from that second. She was life itself.

Just for that one moment you haven't got another thought in the world. Everything stops. It's a short-lived memory and things snap back into reality. But it's almost like when they slow down a part in a film to give extra effect. This happens in reality and gives the same effect.

You realise then how precious life is and how you should respect it. Your feelings on life and the way that the world is changes...You drive slower you take life at a slower pace, you love life and everything in it, and then sympathise with every problem that other people have with their families where as before you would just be courteous and say ah never mind but not really give a damn.

My daughter was born in the summer and unusually for this country it was very hot. Typically the hospital didn't have any air conditioning and was extremely hot. As if giving birth wasn't bad enough my wife was trying to cope with the heat. She hated staying in the Hospital and wanted to come home straight away, but the nurse explained that they had to stay in just so they could keep an eye on mother and baby until the next day. My wife called me very early the next day very stressed and upset as she hadn't been able to get any sleep and just wanted to come home. So I rushed over to the hospital and collected the two most precious things in my life. Its kind of weird but all I can remember about that day is when we got into the car and left the hospital the song Life by desiree came onto the Radio. I can't hear that song anymore without thinking of taking home my baby who was just about 24 hours old.

After the Birth I had noticed a change in my wife it was subtle things at first and i put it down to the after affects of childbirth, yet noticed after a while that things were becoming more than that and she was changing a lot. I tried to be gentle about asking and would ask if there was anything that I could do or help with. But soon it got worse and asked her to go to the Doctors, she said that if it persisted then she would.

Things didn't get any better but had seemed to remain on a certain level and my wife had said that it would be all right soon. I plodded on in terms of the relationship tense as it was believing that the two of us were strong and that it would soon sort itself out. After all this should be one of the happiest times in our lives with our new baby. I was still floating on cloud nine; I had a baby daughter and had to tell everyone. The only downside to all of my happiness was that my wife was constantly tired snappy and grumpy. She had a lot of trouble with her family too. They had always done something to annoy her. They were simply selfish in many respects. It was like oh yeah wow another baby great. I was slightly shocked too at their lack of attention to their first and only grandchild. My mother in law actually planned her holiday so that she was away for the birth.

"You wont want me around" she said to my wife…

I just thought that it was strange. I know that in years to come if my daughter is going to have a baby I will move heaven and earth to be there for her. Thing is though my wife and her Mother have always had a funny relationship. Many times we had left her parents house and my wife would be in tears complaining about the way her Mum had both spoken and treated her. In the end I just got used to it.

But not being there at the birth of their first grandchild I thought was very bad.

I also remember when the rest of her family came down two days later that they didn't even bring a card to congratulate us. I mean who turns up to visit for the first time their Very First Granddaughter or niece even their Great-grandchild without so much as a card??? Well this lot did. I just couldn't believe it. That had to top it all off. And of course as soon they were out the door my wife got upset and I was left trying to explain that she should know by now what they are like. Still it didn't make it any easier on her, the one time in her life when she needed all the support that she should get from her family and they weren't there.

But we managed to get by with life and the dramatic wonderful change that we had in our lives Five short months after our daughters birth however my life was to change dramatically and I shall never forget it for the rest of my life, and one other thing constantly reminded me of that fact.

That Bloody Yucca plant!

We had just passed Valentines day which was the usual exchange of cards Husband to Wife and I remember reading the card that my wife gave me telling me that she would always love me even though sometimes she wasn't always great at showing it, I knew that she was referring to the recent difficult times that we were experiencing since the birth but remember feeling all warm inside when I read the card and realised that she still loved me very much and was reassured by that card and felt secure and that her feelings for me were re-confirmed that she indeed still loved me.

They are difficult times when you don't receive feelings of love back and feel insecure. Most of the time if two people really are in love there is a bloody good reason as to why they might be a bit off. Considering what my wife had just been through I think that she had more than enough reasons to be a bit different.

I remember leaving work a few days later with a Yucca plant that somebody had ripped out of somebody's Garden after a drunken night on the town whilst staggering home during the weekend and had dropped it off outside the offices where I worked. Knowing how my wife liked plants like that I thought she would like it if I took it home for her. As I walked in the front door I showed her the gift that I had rescued for her which she seemed very happy with but there was something strange about her an air that I hadn't seen before and she asked me if she could talk to me, sure I said so I sat down at our kitchen table, all ears.

Now ever since that day those words stuck in my mind and the look on her face. I think that it is now etched permanently into my brain as a warning sign for possible danger. Had I known what was about to happen I would have run for the door and bolted...never to return. If you should ever be unfortunate enough to hear similar words, which are followed by a very uneasy feeling inside you gut...then prepare yourself.

Its very weird how your own personal psyche knows that something bad is coming but is unable to prepare you for what it is. Kind of like your mind is telling your body…hang on something shitty is on the way but im dammed if I know what it is…you best just prepare yourself for the worst…..

The Worst as it was came yet nothing in the World could have ever prepared me for what she was about to say and I shall remember it for as long as my memory still is intact.

I sat there knowing that there was something wrong and that whatever she was going to say was troubling her in quite a way because she was finding it difficult to communicate with me. This wasn't like her we could normally talk quite easily and never went round in circles like this. I started to feel uneasy and as my sixth sense was picking something up, my stomach started to twist and turn and a numbness was creating in my gut, something wasn't right, but surely it couldn't be that bad, could it. Time seemed to just stop and I can still picture her now sat opposite me with her head down and she was playing with her nails concentrating on something but what was it. I didn't want to speak in case I forced her in to saying something and it wasn't something that I wanted to hear, I mean after all no news is good news right?

I have always been one who would rather wait for an eternity for news if it was bad in the hope that whilst waiting it would force the news into not so bad news. God this was killing me, I was beginning to sweat but I couldn't ask her, I couldn't push her she had to speak…. …Then she did.

I'm not happy and I don't love you anymore!!!!

It is one of those times when you hear somebody say something but don't really register what they have said, I sat there in silence looking at my wife, and felt completely numb, waiting for her to say oh I was only joking, but after waiting for a while I went from a numb state of shock to a panic mode that seemed to go into overdrive. The punch line to this joke that I was praying for with my whole body just didn't come. There is no way on Earth to describe that instantaneous feeling that you have. They only way for someone to know how you felt is to have gone through it. There is no preparation for this…no course you can take…. no magical pill that makes it all go away…(Though some of my friends might disagree with me there.)

It's a pain that you have to experience first hand to fully know where I was at.

"W-w-w-w- what do you mean?"

"I'm sorry, I really am, its nothing that you have done, Its me….don't blame yours.."

"What the hell do you mean, you don't love me anymore? What are you saying…I thought that…"

"Look I'm sorry I just don't feel very happy, ever since the birth I haven't felt right…"

"Why haven't you said anything before, I thought that you were feeling better? What are you saying?"

At this stage I began to feel very sick inside and panic set into my voice and my heart was beating hard against my chest and I couldn't think straight. My whole world was coming down and I couldn't do anything about it. Things in my head were spinning, what should I say what should I do, this cant happen, she doesn't mean it, this is ok, it can be fixed she's just upset about something, think what have you done, what can you change…

"When did all of this start?. How? I mean…why…what do you want me to do? I cant understand why you are unhappy?
"

"Look it's just me and I can't really explain why…it's just that I've changed…"

"Why cant we just talk about this, I think that you've over reacted, and there must be some way that we can work this out, surely?"

"Look I just can't see this working, but you must understand that it's not you, it's me"

Holy fuck, then I suddenly realised about my daughter!!

"What about the baby, what's going to happen"

"Look she will be fine but I need to also try and get myself back together aswell, maybe I just need a break from all this, I just don't know what has happened."

"Oh that's just fucking great, so what am I supposed to do?"

"I'm so sorry I just don't know anything anymore, just that something's wrong and I am not happy.!"

No matter how many times we went over it, I had to admit to myself that everything that I was saying and thinking was just clutching at straws. It eventually dawned on me that nothing that was going to change her mind about this, and just started to think that she just needs a break and soon it will all be ok.

I can remember sitting their for the rest of the evening talking to my wife about what we were going to do, trying to make all of the conversations upbeat and positive on my side, in the hope that she would think ah, look he's really trying and maybe everything will be ok. So I started to say that yes, I'll be ok if you go, hey life's wonderful. I can't really remember much of what I said after that but know that I was talking and walking about in circles for ages. It was as if something inside my head had switched off or snapped.

It was as if I wasn't thinking and someone else had come in and taken charge of me. I felt great though as if I was a bit drunk. What am I so worried about? It was a moving experience as I can remember thinking that my wife is going to leave me and take my daughter yet it was as if I couldn't register what that truly meant.

I was there rabbeting on for ages, making no real sense at all, to the point that an hour later after I had moved the furniture around in the dinning room twice trying to make the room seem more spacious. I think that there is a madness part of the brain that makes you perform really stupid simple tasks to take your mind off the situation, like in films when you see somebody cleaning the silver or polishing windows when they have been told of somebody's death. It's a bizarre feeling, something inside does take over, you keep wanting to cry and collapse on the floor in a heap, end it all destroy yourself, or wake up from this nightmare but something inside really has taken over and prevents you from these self destruct modes.

I can remember standing there wondering what to move next, yet still unable to think about the severity of what had just happened in my life yet my mind wouldn't let me go there, it really was protecting me. That is amazing how the mind looks after you. There is probably a long winded medical word for it "Loopy" seems about right though as I couldn't control my emotions, I had gone on to auto pilot. I would possibly like to know what and why that happens as I m sure someone somewhere can tell me. The thing is though he or she would probably tell me that I had answered it myself.

Then just like in the films it hits you, from nowhere, I was pushing the glass's cabinet across the dinning room and then just started hysterically crying, I fell to my knee's still clutching up onto the cabinet as if I was hanging off a cliff. I couldn't let go…this was keeping me from the inevitable…then I started speaking fluent gibberish, mouth wide open with incomprehensible sounds oozing from the pit of my stomach, the feeling of emotionally pain had set in and

I couldn't stop for love nor money it just keeps coming and coming.

Stopping doesn't even come into range of thoughts when you are grieving uncontrollably and it is going to carry on until you physically cant or your mind decides that it has had enough. Similar to before when the mind protects you, it appears now as if the mind has lost a battle with the emotional part of your brain.

You have seen it on the TV and it just looks as though they are in some sort of pain. Well when you have been there in the same emotional experience you can sympathise with them, note the pain and agree with them. Your mind takes you back to that time when you were like it. You remember it for a split second or two them your mind closes the door on that one as if to say 'Ok that's enough of that, we don't want to be opening up that corner of your mind thank you very much' and you come back to life. I'm sure that one day I will be able to look back on all of this and reflect on it, but why would I want to do that.

I don't really suppose that I need to go there again, I only ever go there for myself. For instance whilst writing this down for you now I have to visit it in my mind and its not a nice thing to do. In all honesty I don't believe that I will ever get over what happened. I think that you just learn to deal with things and put them away in a deep corner of your mind. Im sure that over time it will ease and I wont think about it so much.

It really is one of the most horrific feelings that I have ever been put through in my entire life. It's a virginal pain that I hadn't felt before and don't ever want to feel again in this lifetime or any bloody other. I can remember then running up the stairs and taking all of her clothes out of the wardrobe and throwing them into a suitcase, saying well if your going to go then just bloody go now, then I spotted her wedding dress that had been hanging up in the spare room for since the wedding,

"Ha what a fucking waste of time that was"

"Look please stop, this isn't good for you, please st...."

"What do you care, you don't give a shit about me, what are you still doing here, get out"

"Please just come and talk about it"

"Piss off, just get out."

I can still remember then holding on to the top of the wardrobe and collapsing inside again speaking fluent pain and crying without breathing or making any noises, dribble just falling out of your mouth, but hey who really care what you look like when someone has just ripped out your heart, your dreams, your life together that you had planned..........who gives a shit, who really gives a shit!

To put down the correct words that can make anyone in the world understand the true feelings that overcome you when you have destroying news such as that, is so very difficult, in fact it is damn near impossible. Its like when you hear of a death of a close friend or family member, its so hard to describe what happens inside. Its an unknown element of the human emotion that unprofessional people like you and me couldn't put into words.

The feeling of complete uselessness slowly compressed all of my heart and chest and I had trouble in gaining the power to collect normal thoughts. You know that you're in pain but you keep trying to figure out why? That's what really starts to kick you in the balls, why? What have you done to deserve this?

The last recollection I have of that day was wondering about the house late at night when my wife was asleep, and wondering into my little girl's room. Looking at her in her cot, her chest slowly moving up and down with her breathing, slow movements of her feet and hands, I tucked her in and kissed her ever so gently on the forehead.

Then it suddenly dawned on me this was about to get a thousand times worse for she would probably take away my little girl, I remember sitting down on the floor level with the cot and I could see her through the bars in the cot, I was just watching her, then realising what was about to happen, I began to cry, sob, desperately trying to keep the noise in, praying to God "Please don't take my baby away, please don't take my baby away, please help us work this out, please God Please..."

The Next couple of days were a complete blur and bloody awful. I hope and prayed that something would happen and she would change her mind. It was like living on egg shells every second of everyday. Please let something change inside her…make her change her mind…why was this happening to me? What was going on here?

Then the day of reckoning came and my wife moved out, and took my baby daughter, I stood rigid brave as a warrior about to enter into battle, keeping inside the feelings of pain that were raging through my entire body. Inside I was screaming at the top of my voice…. but no one was listening to me. .i can tell you that I have never felt as lonely at that moment in my life…nothing and nobody would or could help me…it was just me…. on my doorstep awaiting the departure of her car, as it drove away I felt nothing………….i had no thought's or feelings for those few cold seconds as if somebody had put the world on pause and the only thing moving was her car leaving the street.

My wife was crying and never looked at me, my daughter sat in her car seat in her little world of normality looking out of the window. As the car disappeared around the corner it was as if somebody just pushed play again on the worlds video and I began to hear the people over the road, I turned and went inside the house, shut the door and collapsed against it and slid to the floor………again tears and fluent pain returned as I knew that they would and knew that this time it was going to be a very, very long time before they went away. This was a pain that was here to stay, how the fuck was I going to get through this?

No Choice:

On reflection of that fateful day one of the worst things that happens inside is when the women leave 's the man for no apparent reason, and when children are involved there is absolutely nothing that a man can do about her leaving with the child.

The feeling of uselessness is so very great that you begin to despise the law. We are told what is going to happen and there isn't a fucking God damn thing that we can do about it…we have no choice, the choices are all made for us…that is so unfair, and I think that something should be done about it. Why is it that I, who had done nothing wrong, in my marriage or after the birth of my daughter, am told that look sir your wife has left for her own reasons and wants to live

117

somewhere else, oh and she is taking your daughter and there is nothing that you can do about it.

I think the person who made that rule should be made to go through the same pain. You don't care about being fair or nice or kind all you want is your child back. Why should my relationship with my daughter be changed in anyway because the Mother feels different? Fine if you feel different Fuckoff and live in a hole somewhere but leave my daughter with me.

The Loneliness:

That night I can remember just trying to get on with things in my own way, trying to forget what had just happened and just kept the thought that we'll sort all of this out and she'll come back soon with my little girl when she's feeling better. I wandered about like a puppy when its left all alone in the day, moving furniture and cleaning up, humming tunes and trying to stay calm, TV. I thought, that would calm me down.

Whoops what a bloody mistake...Why is it that as soon as there is a personal emotional problem in your life, as soon as you watch normal TV. Somebody in the soaps is going through exactly the same thing as you, his wife is leaving, he's lost his daughter etc etc...well that was enough there I was crying my heart out again. It was like a twister and you had very little notice that it was coming. The slightest thing on the TV would start you off. A commercial for nappies would come on and that was it immediately tears would start pouring out of my eyes, sobbing to the point where it looked as though I was jumping up and down on a pogo stick trying to contain the tears.

It didn't last long though and I would have a quick reality check with my self and a little self pep talk, 'Come on you'll be ok you wait and see she'll be back soon, everything will be ok. She just needs a little bit of time away then she will realise how much your meant to be together and come home.' It is very weird how the human body copes with things and how it is then different for different people. Some have a way of holding emotion inside not showing anything, hiding it. Myself on the other hand well that is a different matter. These passing's of emotions were frequent but thankfully they didn't last for very long. The thing was that I knew these feelings weren't going to go away very quickly. Oh I hoped and prayed that soon everything would be alright but as the days turned into weeks I knew that things were going to get worse before they were going to event think about getting better.

Over the next few days I had to try and have the persona that everything was ok in the world and that everything was normal. Work was a blur and to this day I don't know how I managed to get through it each day. It was killing me to try and pretend that all was ok at home. I would hope for busy times when I would be able to forget for a hour or so about all of the shit that had just been dumped on my life. I can remember trying to find excuses to ring my estranged wife so that I could talk to her and hope that she would say something like,

"I want to come back...I'm lonely"

But she didn't, and then I would feel worse. Although I looked after my Daughter everyother night, it still took so much to get through each day when I wasn't able to look after her. So I knew that I had to get out and see people Surround yourself in friends as they advise, but each night I'd get home and just want to curl up and die. It was a horrible existence on the nights when I didn't have my daughter to occupy me. Wondering, thinking, crying all the nights seemed to have the same pattern where I couldn't change anything. I also found that Eating also became too much of a hassle because I didn't feel like it but knew that I had to eat and managed to survive on the bear minimum to keep going, yet it was crap food like sausage rolls and pot noodles, anything that would require the least amount of culinary skills. I remember trying to make an effort for myself and cooking only to find that I would probably eat a quarter of the dinner and just leave the rest, probably heating it up the next day. This proved that there had to be something wrong as up till then I don't think I had ever left anything on my plate, or any other plate at the table. We were brought up to always clear our plates...I guess that transcribes that we are a load of greedy bastards in my family...

One of the worst parts was the lack of sleep, id get to bed and end up just lying there for hours thinking about why she left, when will she come back, and then remember to pray to God asking for her return, because I knew that if I prayed everyday then he would help me and that she would soon return. Yes what a fat lot of good that was, I can remember hating God and blaming him and wanting to know exactly why he had done this to me. Was it divine retribution for all of the young girls hearts that I had broken? Ha I should have been so lucky. I would try to remember of all the bad things in my life that I had ever done, to see if there was one that warranted this pain as a punishment...but I truly haven't done anything that would deserve this revenge.

It was a gut wrenching time, crying, falling half asleep then getting a panic attack, getting up and walking about, it was entirety of loneliness in the night. And it made me feel like shit, going to bed is usually something that you take great delight in as there is usually somebody to go with you that you can cuddle up with or even get rid of some of that testosterone with sexual activities...that's a shag to you and me. Yet in these times for a weird reason all sexual thoughts are completely removed from your head, I would dream about being able to lie there and smell her hair, to stroke her head, that would be better than a marathon of sex.

Having her back in my life would be all I would ever ask for in my entire life. Even a chance would be better than this. I should ask her to come back and stay at the house with me, not as a couple as friends so that I could see my daughter and she would learn to want to be with me again. God I was desperate now anything would be better than this. I just needed her there for a bit longer each day. I would drift off thinking of her there with me cuddling up.

Now that does not sound like a man does it, no thoughts of SEX what's going on???? This should demonstrate to any women reading this that the ending of a relationship can affect a man more that you realise. It put a lot of things into perspective for me at that time. I think that we do take things for granted a lot, and it's only in the bad times of death or a relationship breakdown where we show are true feelings for someone. We would try to overcompensate and do a million things in the time it took to do ten,if only we had another chance.

What can I do?

Once the initial shock was out of the way I started to try and think about how can I solve this, it becomes an obsession like you have never had before, it takes over your every thought again I think its Gods way of helping you cope with it, he gives you false hope and something to hang on to, you can never see it at the time, but it is over and everyone else it trying to tell you, look she's gone forget it just let go and get on with your life as it is now, I can remember my father later on saying at one point.

"Look its been 6 Months if she was going to come back she would have by now, you have to get on with your life, tell her, either you come back right now or forget it."

Of course he was right but at the time you agree with him but do nothing about it, I'll just give it a little more time, just a bit more she will come around soon and want o be back together. She just needs a reality check and to see how hard life is on your own, its tough out there and we had it good together she will soon realise that we are supposed to be together and will be soon.

It then dawned on me that I should get her to a doctor because she kept saying that there was something wrong since the birth of our daughter so I started to investigate the possible area of what could possibly be wrong, postnatal depression maybe that was the answer and asked my wife to go to the Doctor to see if this in deed was the problem. I can remember feeling as though there was light at the end of the tunnel, when I asked her she wasn't happy but eventually went with me, so we sat there and explained the symptoms and he recommended help from a councillor and then my wife agreed to go.

It felt so awkward sitting there trying to explain to the Doctor why we were actually there, I had to do the majority of the talking and I soon became aware that the Doctor had figured out for himself that my wife was not happy to be there and soon asked me to let my wife please answer his questions. It was like pulling teeth getting answers from her but eventually she admitted to him that she didn't feel quite herself…(God that was a fucking understatement of the century). He kept questioning her about the symptoms and her feelings emotionally then agreed that she should see somebody.

It turned out to be a physiotherapist, and in some ways it made me feel better because I thought that at last we have found that there is something wrong and that we would have a chance to get back together once my wife had got to see someone. I had some hope and felt a lot better in the fact that now things were going in the right direction, and at last there would be a reasonable explanation for all of this, some simple cure a few tablets and a few months then we could slowly get back to normal life where we were all happy and together again as a family. This for some time gave me hope and something to be positive about. I can remember instantly having room to breathe and a bit of normality entered my life again.

I would speak to my wife about the sessions that she had with the Psychotherapist, she said that sometimes he made her feel better yet other times it made her feel worse because of what he made her go over whilst talking to him, questions about me and her, I asked if I could go but he had told her that it would require different counselling for that as a couple and that he wouldn't do that, or at least that is what she told me.

Work got better for a while and life was becoming bearable again and I found that I could start to discuss it with family and friends because I had a bit of hope, until now I hadn't told anyone. But thought that I should talk to my family about it but didn't know how!

My wife and I continued to talk every night about the problem and things seemed to get better for a while.

I was then able to go out again with friends socially and drink with them and not be to worried about getting upset when drunk. The problem when drinking if you are depressed is that it makes you feel much worse. It almost highlights the emotional state that your in so I don't recommend having heavy drinking sessions if you are a little depressed.

Eating also became a regular pastime again for me and slowly things started to get back on track.

I can still remember though that the slightest thing could set me off crying and collapsing for a good few hours, a simple advert of babies on the television would remind me again that my daughter wasn't there to cuddle or put to bed or bath, the really simple things that most of married couples take for granted or see as a nuisance which admittedly they do get on your nerves at first because it breaks your routine, yet you really don't mind doing them because of the amount of love that a new born baby gives you. I would stand in the doorway of her bedroom and look at her cot and get upset because she wasn't there to check on or listen too.

It is such a hard thing to do, even now to this day I miss my daughter terribly when she is not with me, but at least now I'm not a snivelling wreck on the floor crying for bloody Europe screaming incoherently at God and asking what the hell did I do that was so bad to deserve this. It occasionally crosses my mind now but its seconds long and found that the best cure for that is to switch it off. Its difficult not to think about her but that is the way that I have to deal with it right now. I just have to blank her or I start to get upset again. Of course I don't mean memories of her or saying her name, just the visualising scenes in my head of us playing, those I have to block when she's not with me.

After weeks of therapy things still hadn't changed in my marriage, my wife had now moved to a house on an estate which was horrible, she showed me the house and I couldn't show happiness, I guess that even if it was Buckingham palace I would have showed disapproval just because it wasn't our family house. It was in a bad area but the house was much better than where she was at the moment, at least my daughter would have her own bedroom and enough room to run around. My Daughter was growing up quickly through all of this and that made up a bit for the pain I had because the time that I had her became a wonderful experience each day with new words and expressions that made me both laugh out loud and then also hold her an try to contain the tears and sadness that were inside because I knew that she was only with me fifty percent of the time.

I remember at one stage telephoning and speaking with the Midwife who was lovely and tried to tell me nicely that it wasn't her job once the baby had been born to talk with my wife, and told me that she would call the lady at the doctors who would call her and try to help with the situation, the midwife explained that she could loose her job if she was to talk to my wife and discuss with her the problems, why they make that stupid rule I still to this day don't understand, surely if there is a person in need of help then does it really matter who the hell speaks to her? Well apparently so, it just seemed that whoever I spoke to I just kept getting passed around because it was too much trouble, and even then the other lady took ages to call, and left a message once, and of course my wife didn't want to ring back because she said that the women was rude to her before, and they don't chase things up, no matter how many times I rang they said that it was my wife responsibility to call her back, "you cant make a horse drink and all that" bollocks, my wife needed help and I couldn't find anybody to help.

Well that was my belief, and so I carried on, they said that they were slightly concerned about her after the birth and suggest that she call the hospital about post natal depression and left it up to her, well I'm sorry but that just sucks, yet I could see there reasoning but at the time just feels like nobody could give a shit. The problem is though admittedly I never knew what my wife was telling them and if she was telling me the truth!!!

I think that it gets to the point then where people don't want to ask you what's going on for fear of upsetting you anymore. My friends and family were fantastic all of the way through, they learned to let me get on with it and just asked every now and then if I ever needed anything, just tell them. You never do, but if I was ever in that situation again or anyone who is reading this is then I tell you now for god sake tell somebody, everybody absolutely everything, blurt it all out get it out of your system, call her a fucking old bitch, scream, cry explode, and you do feel better after it, you really do. It all seems doom and gloom when your in it, but hey that is reality it is fucking shit and you do feel like there is nothing inside, your whole life as you know it has ended, but you will get through it no matter how bad it is remember that you really will, I did and you will.

I wont be the last by a long way. You think at the time that there is nobody in the whole world that understands your pain, your grief, and nobody will convince you other wise, of course you know that there are children and people dying everyday but right now you don't care it is your survival and your life that you want back. It takes a while longer than you think but trust me, from one who knows you will get better and one day laugh at what a stupid bastard that you must have looked led there snot everywhere, you'll never forget it but it will pass. It's a hard thing to admit to people that you sat there talking out loud to yourself and kept crying at the slightest thing. But it's the truth and what happened to me...so I'm not ashamed.

The summer came and everyone else was in happy summer mode, and then I met a great girl. It was that last bloody thing on my mind. She was a friend but we were attracted to one another. She knew all of my problems and was a great shoulder to cry on, and the poor cow sometimes had to sit and listen to me for hours going on about all of the shit in my life, I'm surprised that she bothered calling after a while. We became a bit closer than friends and occasionally we saw each other. I'll admit that I liked her, but couldn't commit anything to her because I had that thought that at any moment my wife could want to get back together and so that stopped things going anywhere. I can remember thinking that if I had had a relationship with her and that if I did get back with my wife and had to tell her then she would change her mind and not get back with me because I had been with someone else.

This became apparent to my friend because she told me that we couldn't go out together as a couple for she feared that I would get back with my wife. I think that I tried to tell her that this wouldn't happen because I didn't know if I wanted to see her or not, but this was hardly fair on her and knew deep in the back of my mind that she was right and she knew it too. Gladly though we still remained friends to this day.

A little while after the summer my wife and I saw even more of eachother and did have laughs amid the sadness. But as usual I had to spoil it by asking questions all of the time, I had to every now and then ask her what were we doing, were we going to get back together, would it be soon, did she miss me or us still I always got the answer,

"Well maybe, I don't know."

What a cliff hanger, so id change the subject and try again to carry on letting things get better as they seemed to be in my eyes. I even asked her whether she was seeing anybody or not, "Of course not, do you think that I would have anytime or thought for anybody else at the moment the way I feel that's the very last thing on my mind…."

Bollocks I thought in the back of my mind, but at the same time wanting to believe her so much that I did, and felt happy with the words that she had told me, and she convinced me that she wasn't.

I couldn't bare the thought if her being with anybody else. You have these thoughts and conjour up mental images of her with someone else. These are obviously emotionally damaging thoughts and you end up fighting against these thoughts. Only problem is that the more that you fight it the more that you think about it.

Another few months went by and things between me and my wife began to get a bit better, she even stayed around a few times to watch videos etc… and she stayed at the house in the same bed, which was great although there was no physical contact we slept together and as far as I was concerned that was better that sleeping alone and not having her there. Strange but better. It is a totally weird concept to sleep in a bed with your wife and have absolutely no physical contact. I would just lie there and hope that she would want a cuddle or ask me to hold her, but she didn't. I started to imagine us being as close as we were before and I could even smell her and hear her breathing. That was just absolute torture to me and I know that it would be just as bad for anybody else. I don't know if you have ever had that scenario but I wouldn't advise it if you haven't.

A few weeks after that my wife asked if she could come back and give us another go.................

I couldn't fucking believe it, my prayers every night had been answered I was on top of the world, he words sent me into the next fucking dimension, and I accepted her very kind request with open arms. I really thought that this was the turning point and just couldn't believe that this nightmare was finally over. I had dreamed about this day for so very long and was determined that this time everything was going to be perfect. I would make sure that everything that we had ever talked about doing we would do. Having my daughter back was the biggest thing to me. I had missed her so very much and now I would have her back in my life 24 hours a day 7 days a week.

When you loose something so very close to you your world ends inside and all that you do is remember how things were. I was so lucky because now I would be able to have all that I had been remembering for the past months back again. It was as if I had been granted a wish and it had come true. Finding yourself in a situation as this through no fault of your own always makes you doubt the kind of person that you are. Didn't you do enough of this or that, why had this happened? You just end up going around in circles in your head and it does have a knock on effect with the rest of your daily routine. For me I had always tried in my life to be the best that I could.

Treat others as you wish to be treated. My father has always said to live life to your own standards and never stoop to those who are beneath that standard. But things like this knock your own self-esteem and you find yourself doubting the person that you are. Then it all changes and with my wife coming back into my life and my baby girl I knew that it wasn't all bad and that I must have been just worrying too much.

So here we were back to normal, well sort off and at least it was a beginning to a new start and eventually I was getting back to normal, well almost, hey I didn't care how long this took as my wife and baby girl were back with me, I couldn't have been happier. My family and friends were all very happy for me; I had my bounce back immediately. It was a bit strange at first with us sleeping in the same bed with nothing happening in the sex department, but my wife said "look don't worry it will just take time" we tried a kiss once but it to be honest was really shit, kind of like kissing your own hand, and even then you felt rejected by your own hand, she tried to laugh it off and said not to worry, but something kicked me in the nuts and said oh come on, if you wanted to get back with somebody that you loved and had had a child with who you'd been apart from for almost 8 months then the first thing that you would want to do is get into bed with eachother and show that you still fancied eachother.! Maybe that's just me or something.

The next thing was that I heard her on the phone to one of her friends whilst I was checking on my daughter the next night, and could hear my wife's end of the conversation, with her saying.

"Yes I have, and I think its for the safety and security that's why, but it will be ok I think…"

Those words made me feel very insecure and sad again. I mean what a shitty thing to say. All I could hear was her words repeating over and over as to why she had come back. Safety and Security. What a crock of shit. That is just a way of saying that it was the easy thing to do. All that I could think then was that she didn't come back for me or for a close family life. It wasn't out of love or the fact that she missed me it was just for Safety and Security. Jesus, did I confront her about this or just pretend that I hadn't heard her? Surely if I pretended that I hadn't heard it overtime it would just bug me and make me a bit of a walk over and one of those under the thumb husbands who jumped every time that there wife shouted. I couldn't live my life as a lie. I had to bring it up with her; this was too big an issue to leave festering in my mind.

When I asked my wife about this she just almost repeated the same thing to me saying that her friend was very happy we were together again, and her friend had asked her what made her go back, and she told her what I had heard, it pissed me off and I told my wife, but probably with less venom than what I actually felt inside, I mean I didn't want to scare her off as she had only just returned. So I carried on.

The next day my wife rang and said that she wouldn't be around until about 7-7.30 as she was going to go back to her house and clean out my daughters rabbit! Ok I said and went home. When my wife came home about 8 with some reason for being late that the rabbit had escaped, then she went straight up stairs for a shower!!!!

Suspicious? Me, of course I fucking was, my mind went into overdrive.........why would she want a shower after cleaning a rabbit out, cant it wait until after dinner I asked, I wont be long she said, and went up. Hmmmmmmmmmmmm.

That would have been ok if it hadn't happened the same time two days later on. Then I was convinced that she was meeting someone at her house having sex with them forgetting the fucking rabbit and then coming home. So I followed her up stairs very quietly and listened to her because I thought that she was checking on our daughter and talking to her, when I reached the top of the stairs I realised that she wasn't in there she was in the bathroom on her mobile phone. She later denied that she was and asked what I was doing creeping about and listening at doors for her.

I began to feel sick again and an enormous feeling of mistrust came over me. She later on said that she was going to check on our daughter, she was gone a while and I could hear her messing about on her mobile scrolling through the menu and hearing the beeping noises that it makes. I crept up the stairs and paused half way trying to hear what she was doing, she was sending a text message as I could hear the keys being punched out, then as I knelt on the stairs listening I turned slightly and saw a remarkably sad sight. I will never forget to this day.

It was me in the mirror, I could see myself through the stairs and looked at myself and thought, what the fucking hell are you doing creeping about In your own house listening to your wife who you wanted back in your life so much because you don't trust her, how sad have you become. With that thought I turned and went back downstairs. When my wife came back down stairs I asked if our daughter was ok, she said that she was fine but she thought she was going to wake up so she watched her for a while. I again never said anything.

As the week neared an end my wives real Father wanted to come up and visit to see our daughter, ok I said but I wasn't ready I didn't think I wanted to see him again so soon, I guess that it was out of embarrassment I suppose so I declined the offer and said that I would go and see my sister and her kids that weekend and maybe go and see some friends on the Saturday, this seemed to be to my wives delight!

On the Sunday she said that she was going to stay at her place as she had load s of washing and things to do, I said that she could do it all at my house but she said that she wanted to clean etc.. so we arranged that I would have my daughter on the Sunday night when her Father had gone and that she would bring our daughter around at about 5,30. Ok no problem.

140

The Bread Man!!

On the Sunday night my wife rang at about 5 and said that she would bring our daughter to me and save me driving out to her house as her Father was just leaving, ok no problem, so I sat back down again as I was just getting ready to go and collect our daughter.

About 5 minutes later the phone rang so I answered but there was nobody on the other end, but I knew that the line was connected to someone., I was just about to put the phone down when I could hear my daughter laughing and making noises down the phone I could also hear my wives voice in the background calling my daughter. I listened for a while and was laughing to myself imagining my daughter on the floor playing with the phone because she had obviously pushed the redial button.

I was waiting for my wife to discover her in the hall on the floor playing with the phone.

After a few minutes I was going to hang up but then everything in my life changed.

"We have run out of bread, could you bring some with you when you come back, I'll give you some money!"

"No don't worry silly, I'll get it "said my wife to the strange male voice.........................
I suddenly realised that my wife was talking to a man. A man…. but …who the fuck was he?

"Fuck, fuck, fuck, is all that was going on in my head…
"Hello…Hello…hello!" It was my wives voice/.
"Who the fuck is that………….."!
All that followed was an awkward silence, which seemed to go on forever….
"Who was it" I asked again…

"Who, what ummmm..its just a friend…….." she was lying through her teeth….and she was panicking I could hear it in her voice.

" I think that you better get here right now!"
"Why…what's the problem…he's just a neighbour"

"So what is he a friend or a neighbour"....i screamed,

"Its just one of my candidates from work...he erm.... popped in for a cup of tea...!"

"Friend, neighbour, candidate when are you going to get your story straight?"

I was panicking so much.... is this what I was worrying about all this time...another man...had it come true?

This is where it all started to really go down hill. In seconds I went back to where I was before, lower than ever, I didn't think that it could have got any worse...still something was telling me that it had just started to get worse. Know I knew that my whole world just ended! Just a friend my fucking arse...she had got somebody else. Did she really expect me to believe that!!

I can remember just walking in circles pacing up and down I couldn't sit still, it just kept gong around in my head what that strange male voice had said over and over again. Who was it, fuck, I couldn't sit still...it was as if I had just done something terrible no no no no I kept repeating to myself, God no please don't let this be happening I thought that this was all ok, no please don't do this to me no no, but it kept going around in my head, his words then my wives words, fucking bread!!!! Please don't let me find out like this all over a loaf of fucking bread no, no...

143

It seemed an eternity between the conversation and my wife turning up, it was a paused moment, I was now finding it hard just to concentrate on breathing for the time being. BREAD fucking bread, my thought were interrupted by the doorbell. There she was my daughter, big smiles, and a leap forward from her mothers arms to mine for a big kiss DADDY…

I was obviously trying to remain calm because my daughter was in the same room as my wife, god I wanted to scream and shout and cry, my fears that she was seeing somebody were correct, I was shaking with fear, still wanting it to not be true. I asked her who the hell was it, she said that it was just a friend from work nothing more, she swore, I hated her, what she was doing, she seemed in a panic, but still protested her innocence. I found myself starting to believe her because I wanted too. I didn't really want to know if she was seeing somebody because that would simply just kill me and any of the thoughts that I had been having about us getting back together. I so wanted to believe her that it was just a friend and then found myself thinking, well it could just be a friend, maybe she is right, though I still pressed her and kept asking her who it was,

"Your seeing somebody aren't you?" I screamed…
"NO, I swear I'm not, he's just a friend." She was still covering up I could tell…

The sad thing is though that I had to believe her, so that all of my dreams would be answered and that my wife would come back home and we could all be a family again. I was so desperate for what she was saying to be true,

"He is a friend and that's all that there is too it."

Then I suddenly thought that's why she didn't want me to collect my daughter from her house because I would have found this stranger there, this so called bloody friend.

I confronted her again..

"That's why you didn't want me to collect her today isn't it, so you could be with that wanker..." god as I looked at her I didn't think that I could hate someone so much that I had loved more than anything....

"That's not true...he just popped in unexpected...." She was almost crying...

"Liar, just go will you and leave me alone once and for all"...I have had just enough of this shit!!

This nightmare was getting worse, yet I still kept convincing myself that it would all be ok, and that soon she would come back and we could all be together again and live life normally as one big happy family, that is all I had ever wanted, a great family, beautiful wife, four children and enough money to give us all what we need and a few treats. I had always wanted nice things, a big house a nice car, holidays, the usual dreams that most people have I suppose, but just as we had all of that and it could have been exactly what I had dreamed off, maybe it still will there is time yet.

She does still love me somewhere. I can remember talking to my wife each day as she came around, the thing is thought if you are the one that has been left, dumped, shit on whatever you want to call it, it is always the hurt one that instigates every conversation, and it doesn't take long before again you asking the same questions as if a routine, "Why did you leave though? When are you coming back? Do you still love me? Is there anything that I can do to make you come back sooner? . It probably drove her insane all the questions, but I had to know all of it, it just wasn't fair.

You find yourself in a really desperate state of mind, the questions you know are really beginning to piss off the other party and when you notice the strain in there face, as if to say "Jesus do we have to always go over the same bloody shit everyday," you back down and back track and find yourself almost apologising for the questions and then overcompensate by asking if they want a cup off tea, or a cigarette, anything to ease the tension, to distract their thoughts.

It seems crazy to outsiders that you talk too, or who see you going through this, putting yourself in turmoil as to when are they coming back, you know that there is a good chance that they may never do that but you block those thoughts out and continually hope for the miracle. You are constantly in search of people that have split up and then re joined successfully and who know say that they just needed space, that was it I thought to myself she just needed space, she will be back soon, and there that's it you have yourself convinced that its just a question of time and she'll come running back. It wont be long.

I can remember later on that night when my wife had gone back to the fucking bread man, how I again tried to be positive think of good things, convince myself that what she had told me about them just being friends was true, and I found myself saying in my own head that it was the case, yep he's just a friend, she is attractive, she is bound to get friends, afterall she did say that he was an ugly git and not her type, so why should I be bothered. Yet it was still there, that little niggle that you get in your head and the heavy feeling that you get in your heart, you just know but you lock it away. It was her reaction and struggling way to find words that seemed to give away a signal that..'uh oh…ive just been caught red handed'. God …what the hell do I do now?

Anybody else that you tell just gives you that look, you know the one, it says "oh you poor Bastard, you know that she is shagging him, you know that he's the one, he's got her now not you, and you have fallen for more of her fucking bullshit, you still cant see it, but if your happy with that belief then I'll stand by you, I will."

God I was a stupid bastard believing all of her bloody shit, but that is what love does for you, it gives you this capacity to listen to lies, know damn well that normally you would have no problem in knowing that they are lies, yet now you believe their tales, because it is what you want to hear. That's why we do it, because its what we want to hear. She could have told me that it was a long lost brother who came to visit her and I probably would have ended up believing her eventually.

It is strange though that you take in these lies and I found out why people say that you can live in denial, because I did, I lived that life, and I know now why people do it, and can understand. You know that other people who know have the right insight, they are saying ' what she's moved out, living on her own, says she's confused, ah she must be shagging somebody else, what a stupid git doesn't he know it, he should just tell her to come back or fuckoff out of his life and stop fucking about with his head.'

Of course you know all of this and say it often enough to other friends about their relationships but when its your one then it all becomes different. When you are truly in deep love with somebody to the point where you would do anything for them, then you refuse to believe that your marriage your bond your soul mate has gone, you just wont believe it until it smacks you in the face like a freight train, even then you would probably try and convince yourself that it is just a faze and that you can get back together and try these things. Even if you walked in on your wife and someone else having sex you can bet the excuses would start flowing too,

"Oh it was the drink and afterall you have been ignoring me!!!!" that's a good one, or

"He tripped"……

Yet I still convinced myself that I knew that she still had feelings for me because why else would she have come back to give it a go again, there are still feelings there and she just had to find them all. I can remember asking her, and would advise the same to any other couple that were thinking of splitting up, if deep down inside you have the smallest of feelings about somebody, if when you saw them you started to get butterflies in your stomach, everyone has a certain way or feeling deep inside if they really like somebody.

Its not like an instant attraction feeling you get when first seeing a person that you know you want to be with, this feeling is one that stays with you in a relationship, and allows you years down the line to look at somebody close to you and miss them even if they are not there for a few hours, to feel slightly disjointed when that person is not there, 99 % of the time you don't even give it a second thought, but if you can look at them and there is the tiniest of feelings still there, then grab it by the neck pull it out into your mind and try to build on it, give it a really good go though, run with it, its worth it isn't it.

I kept saying this to my wife…

"Isn't it worth it? Surely it is, we can't just throw all of this away…."

Why give up all of the time that we have had to try something else, someone else, why do that to yourself? Because I tell you now, when you separate if there is the smallest of feelings, as you spend more time away that small feeling gets bigger and bigger and you start to miss that person.

But at the same time there feelings go away a little at a time, so don't do it to yourself, because where ever you go the one you leave behind with the small feelings will always be the one that got away from you.

Facing facts:

It takes a long time to actually come to terms with the fact that you have been dumped or left is probably a better way to put it. Do you actually tell anyone, or let it just be a secret for the rest of your life, that way no one will ever know. You actually find that after a while people have worked it out anyway and are just waiting for you to tell them, they are trying to appear not nosey, they all care very much and you know that, but they start to lay off after a while and just wait for you to mention it instead, they feel more comfortable with this I guess. The thing is, it is so very difficult for people to talk with you about it because they do not want to bring it up in case its going to upset you, but believe me the best medicine in the world is just to talk about it and cry your bloody heart out. Forget all of the macho male bullshit phenomenon just let it all go, it really makes you feel better, every man cries remember that.

Family and friends really do help, just by being in a room and saying nothing that helps, I tented to stay at home and not go out, I guess I wanted to wait in just in case she phoned and wanted to chat, I had to be there just in case, but I can tell you it's the worst thing. The T.V. as I said before will always have something on to remind you of what you're going through. Somebody will be getting divorced or separating or anything that is making your life upside down.

Go and see friends or a family member, I know that you don't want to go, but do it, I waited far too long to go and talk to people, or just sit at there house and say nothing, it just breaks up the boring routine that you have of sitting there thinking about the one that you love not being with you and waiting for them to call you every night, when of course they don't. Then just to piss your system up, they might actually ring on the only night that you have gone out in the past 6 months then you get pissed off with yourself for going out, but you have to learn not to be at there beckoned call, which you do place yourself.

Its is easy to say now that I don't, and am not in that same position, but at the time you will do exactly that, and no-matter what anybody says you will still sit there and wait for that phone to call, and you keep convincing yourself that one day it will.

Yet you yourself know that it probably wont. It does eventually ring, but by the time that it happens your mind doesn't care so much, and then you start to realise that they are now phoning a lot more than you ever imagined they would, and find yourself not returning the calls within seconds if you had missed them whilst at the shops buying your pot noodles. Family do help and talking helps. I thought many times about going to my Doctor and chatting with him thinking that maybe I needed help, with either counselling or with anti depressants, after all that is what my wife was now on happy pills she called them and said that they just take the blues away. I probably should have gone, especially now that I was even more in the shit, after she decided to come back and leave again, that did knock me backwards again and set me off crying to the TV again all of the time at the slightest sad storyline.

But I did the sensible bloke thing and didn't go, ha, I think it was that I was worried about the tablets that they give you and didn't want to become reliant on a pill to keep me happy, I wanted to get though it by myself, more of a character test if you like, there's no doubt that it would make me a stronger person??? But would it, I didn't know, I just knew that I didn't want to take the tablets that he may have given me.

So I carried on and decided that I would get through all of this on my own. Some days were far worse that others. I can remember wanting to tell everyone about the Bread man, but then I wouldn't because I kept thinking that when we got back together I didn't want anybody to think that she may have gone off with someone or had a fling with some guy, I think that it was a personal pride thing, not wanting anybody talking when we'd left about,

"Oh do you remember when he told us about that Bread man guy, she was probably shagging him all along and she just kept stringing him along".

That's the paranoia that I had even before anybody every got the chance to say it, and to me that was the best way, I would take that secret with me to the grave, and nobody would ever be able to talk to me about the bread man. Its so crazy the thoughts that I had and I suppose that there are people out there everyday in the same shit state that I was then. It's a bloody awful thing to have to go through, you find yourself no wanting to tell anybody bad things about the person who has left you because you make yourself believe that it could be a kind of a jinx and with the fact that you have told somebody else that it will now make the situation worse for you, God I mean holy shit, like it could get any worse, ha.

Nothing can prepare you for the constant dull ache and sickness feeling that you get when a loved one leaves you. Its weird though because you always find yourself in a personal fight, half of your head is telling you that you don't really give a shit and that you are now much better off without her in your life and that you never ever really liked her anyway, and that sooner or later you would have probably left the cow, but then reality slips into these thoughts and your sensible head argues with the defensive side and you have to admit that you loved her completely and would have don't absolutely anything for her and to have kept your family together.

There are also the constant thoughts that I had on where I had gone wrong and what it was that I must have done. Even though my wife would constantly tell me that it was nothing that I had done and that it was all her fault, I still tried to go over every little thing in my head and justify to myself that she couldn't have left me for the real true person that I am because I am Mr Perfect and everybody loves me and all that I am, so what did I do somewhere along the way that pissed her off that much. Of course she couldn't have left me for no reason, something I did must have been bad, was it a gradual change over a period of time since we married, had I changed, I just didn't know and it was that not knowing that sometimes would drive me mad.

So I had to try and get on with things again, I remember trying all sorts of things to occupy my mind, anything that would help me forget, moving the furniture around that was always a good one, I remember when she first told me that she was leaving each day was just constant pain inside, people have tried over the years through films, books poetry to describe the pain that you feel when your heart is being really hurt and we watch these films read these poems and books and in the moment that we absorb the words or idea we sometimes feel the pain and sympathise with the characters, even shed a tear in a film when its portrayed well, but five ten minutes later the pain has gone, its only when you are in a position like that when you can really understand the power that love over people.

If everybody were to be really truly open with him or herself about how much they felt for a person, then everybody would have a much closer and better relationship. I'm not saying that somepeople do not do this, but I will try and explain what I mean and the power that love really has.

If you could take time everyday and express to the person that is in your life what they mean to you without holding back then at first it would probably make them cry quite easily, it is by no means an easy thing to do, but just imagine it, trying to explain every tiny little detail about them that you love. To take them to the place in their mind that makes them understand how, why and when you first fell in love with them and why it still remains the same. You have to completely open up though, I can remember sitting there and telling my wife how much I missed just smelling her hair, how I missed just waiting for her if she had popped out, how much I felt alone if she wasn't there.

I know that we all joke and tell them that it was nice without them there for an afternoon, and yes sometimes it is nice to have time on your own, some of us can be apart for ages without feeling bad, but if we were all really honest and true we would have to admit that after the initial escape from our loved ones no matter how much they pissed us off sometimes eventually in a short space of time that we really did miss them, I believe that I should have definitely said more, but the problem is that we always think of these things when its too late, or when our partners tell us that we never show them enough emotion or tell them that we love them enough, we are all guilty off that, the trick is to tell them more often why they are so very special, that is the key and the magic that I think we should all one day find.

We all have friends that we think, Jesus why the hell are those two together, she's always moaning about him, he's always moaning about her, why the hell do they bother, yet some people fit together like that, they love each other to bits and they know that deep down and it just sometimes doesn't appear to outsiders that they should be together. I used to really envy and resent other couples when my wife left, thinking but why should they be together, you try to compare them to yourself and think they don't appear to be this or that you just end up finding fault with them because your jealous, but you quickly learn that love has no boundaries and it will happen for a reason, people have said to me "Oh well it clearly wasn't meant to be", what the fuck do they know I used to think, "Its Fate" they would say, "Fuck Fate" I used to think.

I love her and want her back and that is all that matters, but the facts are that you can't force it and nobody ever will.

People do the strangest things when they are in love and for the most bizarre reasons, no matter how stupid they seem after but at the time they are so correct and have such meaning to you. I think that is the reasoning behind the saying "It was a crime of Passion" I do believe in that now, where love can make you do some crazy things to protect or keep what is yours by what ever means, love does make you blind. How do I know, well this is why:

I can think back to one day not so long after the episode with the bread man I was in my Kitchen washing up, as I was gazing out of the window thinking of what I should say to my wife when she phones, when I noticed that Bloody Yucca Plant!!!!!

I remember bringing it home the day that my wife had told me that she didn't love me anymore and wanted to leave, it was like a constant reminder of that day, and I had planted it soon after that in the garden just under the kitchen window so that I could show my wife occasionally the lovely Yucca that I had bought home for her, it reminded me of how I thought that she would like it as I was driving home, it had taken really well and grown quite a lot over the past 6-7 months, Alan Tichmarsh would have been proud of me I thought.,...............but then it hit me, hang on a minute the day I bought that Yucca home was the day that she left…………..hang on…………its bloody jinxed.

Well that was it I was convinced that because I had still got the plant, that was the reason that my wife hadn't come back.(OOOOPPPSS call in the men in the white coats), but I was really convinced. It seemed the perfect answer to me and the only answer. No sooner had I had the thought and I was on my way to the garden to sort out this Bloody Yucca, I entered the garage and picked up the fork and put on my coat and went round to the kitchen window.

It was like a kind of Mexican stand-off I just stood there and looked at the plant…everything seemed to make complete sense it was because of this Fucking Yucca, this stupid fucking plant that my wife hasn't come back, I was totally convinced and I knew that there was only one thing to do…

I jumped on the fork as hard as I could and it sunk easily into the soft earth around the plant, but as I pulled the fork back this bastard was going no-where. The Fork didn't budge, I pulled with all of my strength, straining, and panting to see the bloody thing fly out of the ground, it was moving giving way, here you come you bastard, here we go…but all that happened was the fork bent backwards and didn't even loosen the plant……….FUCK…. FUCK…

I knelt down in the mud and with the remains of the bent fork started to scrape away the earth around the bottom of the plant. This was hard work and I could feel myself getting a little warm and sweat started to run down my back, but I knew that as soon as I had removed this plant that my wife would come back. I decided to grab hold of the trunk and give it a tug, the tug turned into a frustrated frenzy of shaking and swearing, this had very little effect on the tree and I was out of breathe, as I knelt back in the mud for a breather I felt little spots of rain on my head, oh fucking thankyou…that just finishes is off you bastard thankyou very much.

Still I had to get the bloody thing out then everything would return to normal. After another 10 or 15 minutes there was a bit of a trench around this thing but its roots were somewhere in bloody Australia, I was now getting a bit upset with the frustration and knowledge that if I could just get it out of the ground that the jinx would be gone and she would be back. The rain was now pouring and I was soaked with rain and boiling hot under my coat with sweat. The salty sweat stung my eyes, which were also full of tears, and my nose was running heavily but I didn't give a shit because this bastard was coming out like it or not.

I was now some half an hour into it I could see the end nearing, with more violent shakes I could see and feel that I was slowly winning this battle with the Yucca. Still desperate to remove the plant my emotions were very high and I was hot and sweaty, covered in mud all over my hands face and hair, I looked like a drowned rat, but I was winning and laughing almost hysterically to myself through upset and fear. All of a sudden I heard the neighbours back door open, but I didn't look up nothing was going to stop me, and now I was pulling with all of my heart to get this bloody thing out....

"What are you doing? Don't you know it's raining??

Without thinking I snapped

"Course I know its fucking raining"

With that my neighbour just looked at me and I think was about to say something, but looking at this caveman appearance in front of her, with his hair plastered to his head, and face all covered in mud, clearly very upset she must have decided against it and turned and walked away.

I took a deep breath and pulled with everything that I had left in my body, I thought that my arms were going to come out of their sockets, it all seemed to slow down, I was straining that much I could hear my heart pounding, then slowly I could feel it coming out...then a bit more then...bang I was flat on my back in the middle of the lawn staring up at the grey skies, the rain pounding on my face and a bloody Yucca on top of me...i just started laughing aloud, almost hysterically, I had done it, and now she'd come home.

This is how I know for certain that love really does make you do some very strange things, thinking about it now I know how bloody ridiculous it is to even think that a plant could be a jinx and change a course of my life, but at the time it was the perfect solutions to me and that is all that matters and nobody was going to convince me on that say that I was wrong, it certainly then gave me anew lease of hope for us getting back together. And nothing gave me more pleasure than squeezing the bloody Yucca in to the wheelie bin and snapping all of the roots off.

There is no real explanation for what love does to us and it effects us all in different ways. I pulled up to work one day and was trying to hold it together and was snapping at people left right and centre, but trying to hold back the thoughts that my wife could be with the bread man. I had been very careful up to now not to let anybody see me cry except myself in the mirror when telling myself to get a grip on life. My sister asked me something and I upset her by snapping back and immediately felt really bad, but let it drag on for a while before attempting to say sorry. Then later on we went outside for a cigarette, we sat in my car and she was talking to me about my wife and daughter when I just suddenly lost it and uncontrollably started to cry.

Immediately she was upset to trying to find out what it was, I had to tell someone about the bread man and have them tell me that I was being stupid and that he would just be a friend as my wife had said…so after a few minutes I told her, my sister still upset at seeing me like this tried to reassure me that no matter how much of a cow my wife had been that even she knew that she wouldn't have done that to me, that's what I needed and she gave me a great big hug and I began to feel relieved that somebody else knew.

It felt good that somebody else was there for me to talk to about it, and she was wonderful about the whole thing and gave me a great release of the problem, a problem shared and all that. I knew that soon I would have to tell my Mum, I hadn't told her up to know because she worries so much about us all and is very sensitive and I knew that she would worry herself silly about all this, but at the same time felt bad that I had asked my Dad not to tell her, and that meant that they had a secret and that really wasn't fair of me to ask them to do so.

I think it was also the case that I thought we would have been back together by now and would have all blown over. I can remember trying to find out how many people that I had ever know who had split up and got back together again, so I knew that it would be the same for me. It is so weird the things that we hang on to and pretend that they are going to make things all ok again.

I told my Mum later that day and she as I thought immediately got very upset for me. I played it very lightly and told her that we were still very close and that my wife just needed a little space and I think that I had said she'd only been gone a while, trying to make it seem almost like it was just a silly blip on the marriage front. Yet I knew that it had been going on for a lot longer and I was getting very worried but still there was hope.

The pain in my Mum's eyes and the fact that the tears were welling up inside her eyes and she was trying to reassure me that things would be ok. Being on the other end of the conversations that I must have had with people must be hard because there is absolutely nothing that anybody can say to you that will make you feel better about what is going on. I believe that psychiatrists are just there as a sounding board to enable you to have someone to talk to, and no matter what you have to say to them doesn't really matter to them or effect them, so they can remain calm and rational about both sides of the storey.

Problem is you don't give a fuck about the other bitch when your in full anger mode because all that you can remember is how much that the Bitch has hurt you and made your whole world change. I know that other peoples problems may be worse and that there is always someone worse off than you, but the truth is that at that time you don't really give a shit, and just want your own life back, and its destroying you knowing that someone is able to affect you like this.

We can all ask and I'm sure that we have more than once "Why me? What did I do?" Truth is no one knows. The only person who knows the answer to that question is the person that has hurt you and you will probably never know. That maybe best!

My wife and I still spoke everyday on the phone and met every other day in person when she dropped our daughter off, the joke was we talked too much I think. I would go over the same thing day after day, and I could see that it sometimes was really pissing my wife off, but I just had to know why. I remember asking her did she still love me?

"I love you, but I'm not in love with you".... she replied.

I mean come on what the fuck is that all about, I'm sure that we have all had that said to us more than once in our lives, its like the get out of jail card in monopoly, you have to think quickly on your feet, shit what do I say, if I say no there going to break down, so I know I'll leave them guessing and give them some hope. Then a line that I had never heard before came from my wife...

"It's different, I love you like I love my brother"...

To this day hate her for saying that, but I think as time goes on you learn the meaning of that one...she had to love me because we have a daughter together and for the rest of our lives together or not we are going to have this connection. I would then skip over the subject of splitting up and try to be Mr happy and pretend that I was completely ok with the whole situation, thinking that if she can see me back to normal then she would be more interested in coming back and maybe if I appeared to not give a shit that she would come back, almost as if I'd lost interest in her that it would make her want me to be interested. I can tell you, you really have some fucked up thoughts when you have been hurt in the heart.

Some days it would work and I could carry it of and she would say, "oh your in a good mood" or something like "you seem much better recently" but then I would think that this would give her the reason to not feel bad about what she had done. But these moments for me never lasted long and I would soon revert to the snivelling little schoolboy crying in front of her pleading her to come back. I used to look at her through my teary eyes and think how can you be such a cold bloody bitch, all I wanted was a big hug from her and for her to say look it will all be all right one day.

But not on any occasions from when she told me did she hug me or say anything comforting even though I was there in front of her like a blob of jelly falling apart, she was so cold and would just sit there and almost look board staring into space avoiding eye contact with me, and I really hated her for that.

So know my entire family knew and it did feel better to have them to talk to, and I then felt a bad for not talking to them earlier. Some families are very good at these things, and my family are bloody marvellous. One of the great thing to come out of this heartache for me was the fact that I got to know my elder brother as a completely different person too.

Before that I had an elder brother and I would see him frequently but I didn't really know him as I do now. I was quite young when he left home and all I remember about those years was that he was a typical older brother who used to beat me up and pick on me. But over the months I got to know him and grew much closer to him and I really like him as a good friend aswell as an elder brother. He's not the greatest talker but I found another side to him and he would always call and invite me round to see him and his family, and he involved me in his own time at the weekends with his kids, we'd go fishing and stuff like that, and I knew that it was his way of saying look if you ever need to talk I'm here, and I would just like to tell him and his wife that I really love them for that, and a big thankyou. My whole family were great and very supportive and I have always been close to them, but not always said it. I was always closer to my Sister because we are very alike and she was also truly wonderful.

At one stage I told my wife that my family had all offered to speak with her if she wanted to or needed help and she said no at first, but later on said that she would like to. So she went to see my Mum one-day and had a chat. I turned up and collected my daughter and left with a smile and a wave hoping that my Mum and Dad who were both there were able to talk some bloody sense into her and that she would follow me home and all would be back to normal. Well surprise surprise that didn't happen. My Mum and Dad had talked to her about what had been going on and my Mum bless her had even got a booklet on depression for her which she said that she would take away and have a read off. They talked for quite a few hours and I anxiously waited for my Mum to call me.

The News was not what I wanted to hear, and amounted to the same basic bullshit that I had already heard about 100 times now from my wife, that she felt different trapped and bollocks like that. My sister in law also met her and spoke with her one Saturday whilst I was fishing with my brother, I remember sitting there and not really concentrating on what I was doing, remembering that when we first split up I'd gone going fishing and my wife stopped in where we were and bought my daughter to see me, we chatted for a while, again Mr Happy here was trying to be all happy and over the top when she just responded like someone who didn't know me and clearly didn't want to be speaking to me, yet when she left to go back to her friends she gave me a kiss.

Now to normally that would have happened and I wouldn't have given it a second thought because we kissed all the time, as we loved each other. But this time it was probably the first physical contact that we had had in what seemed like an eternity. It really cheered me up and I thought well she must still love me and want to be with me because she kissed me. I asked her a few days later why she did that if she didn't want to be with me and she said

"Oh I thought you'd bring that up, I shouldn't have done that and i regretted it straight away!", oh thanks for that then you bitch I thought. It continued to amaze me again and again at what a cold and mean cow she could be, but yet I still wanted her back.

I was running out of options and people for her to speak to. Its during hard times when you realise just how close your family can be and should be more often, it goes back to what I was saying earlier about telling your partners that you love them more often, I think that the same goes for your family too, We all have our own different ways of showing love I know, and we all do it at different levels, but I think that every now and then we need to tell them just how much that they mean to us, sometimes its embarrassing but we all now that we feel it but who's to say that they know. So tell them.

So by now I was trying to convince myself that I didn't want her back and that I didn't give a bloody shit if she disappeared of the face of the Earth, yet those moments were by no means long enough for me to really start to believe it. Having had her back in the house for the short time that it was and then her going again, and then the Bread man, you could say that things were getting worse, when I thought that they couldn't.

The thing was now Christmas was coming up and I was not looking forward to that, alone, at home sharing the time with my daughter that was going to be pretty shit. I wanted her to be with me all of the time. The problem is when you feel like this you have never had so many offers from friends and family to come around and have dinner and stay over, which is very sweet of them yet you know that your gonna spend the whole time just sat there thinking about the way things used to be and how you want them back, and you just know that someone is going to ask about it all…. meaning well but it just starts you off again.

Concentration during the day at work was becoming easier before but I had the fucking bread man to contend with inside my head and now I had lead myself to believe that he was just a friend or rather she had made me believe that he was that. So she was back in her house and I wanted to sell mine to create a new beginning for us all to be back together in a new house safe and a warm family again. I discussed it with my wife and she agreed that it would probably be better that I sold the big house that I have because she never really liked being in that big house anyway and bought a new smaller one. With this I took it that hey, hangs on, if I buy a new smaller house one that she wants then she will come back!!! Oh well anything was worth a shot now. So I started to look for a new house and people were starting to view mine. It was at least something to take my mind of the usual sit down and cry routine, and I was getting a bit board of the Karaoke scene that I had started to frequent.

Eventually after about 7 couples looking around I had an offer and decided to accept, they were in no rush and that suited me, as I hadn't found anywhere.

I told my wife and she seemed genuinely happy for me and asked if I wanted her to come and look at new houses with me, well I was taken aback by this but of course accepted and so started to view some houses. Over the next few weeks we spent more and more time together over the weekend and in the evenings, we would sit and play with our daughter and surprisingly have a few laughs. Yet sometimes she wouldn't want to stay and make an excuse that she had to go for a run or going to the cinema with a friend from work. Thinking about it then and now she would always go early on the nights that I looked after my daughter, yet she was quite happy to stay for a few hours in the evenings when she was looking after our daughter!!! Strange that isn't it. Yet I always pretended as though it was fine and that it didn't bother me.

Christmas drew very close and I started to plan presents for my wife, because I guess I wanted to shower her with gifts in the hope that it would woo her! Here's a good clue for you, "Money cant buy you love!" and you would do well to remember that. But at the time you couldn't tell me or anyone else that in the same situation. So I bought all of her presents knowing that I really shouldn't be bothering but I wanted to anyway.

We planned to have Christmas lunch together and then my wife was going to her parents, as I had had my daughter overnight on Christmas Eve, which meant that I want going to be too upset as she really cheers me up and is my world. So after visiting my Parents it was home to meet the wife who had volunteered to cook the dinner. It was a nice Christmas lunch until I realised after the meal that she had cooked the Turkey with the Giblets still inside, but we just laughed about it. Then we unwrapped the presents and exchanges the briefest of kisses almost an air kiss, and she left to visit her parents, and I went to my sisters house where the family were meeting up for dinner. This was a good decision as we all had a good laugh playing Who Wants To Be A Millionaire and watching all of the usual repeats on the T.V.

I got very upset at one point and very chocked with the present that my Sister and Parents had bought me, a days racing at Brands Hatch, it is probably the nicest present that anyone has ever bought and it was difficult not to get upset, but that was because of my mental state of mind. And I think that the Men in white coats brigade would have quite happily carried me away most of the time if they had seen the state that I would get myself in on a regular basis. Just to make it worse it was my Birthday the next day and I just wanted it out of the way. I remember my wife calling me and her and her whole family shouting happy Birthday in the background and I just thought you fucking hypocrites!! But it wasn't there fault so that was a bit harsh, but I didn't give a shit.

With the New Year came new hope! Ha..

My wife was spending more and more time around the house now and we were getting on very well and she had even started to call me a few times just for a chat. Had things started to take a turn for the better I wondered. My wife even asked if she could stay around on a couple of occasions saying that she really didn't want to go back to her house as she didn't feel safe there and she didn't like it, so I gladly let her stay.

The Bread man had completely gone from my mind now and we were getting on very well, nights in together watching videos weekends out spending time with our daughter everything was nearly back to normal, oh except the physical side of the relationship, I was still waiting to pass go on that score and I think that I had rooted to the floor worse than that Bloody Yucca, but hey I wasn't going to spoil this for anything, I had gone a year without sex and so I could wait, not that it was on the top of my mind but a kiss here and there wouldn't have hurt. "It will happen, soon" she would say as we joked about the subject.

Next on the romantic calendar was of course Valentines day, a weekend away I thought would be nice, but then my wife informed me that she wanted to go to visit her brother in Scotland for the Weekend with her whole Family as he was in a play or something. For some unknown reason I had a very bad feeling about this and was not happy atall.

173

My wife told me that she was travelling up to Scotland on the Train with her younger sister who didn't want to travel up in the car! This just didn't seem right to me, would I as a parent let my daughter dictate that she wouldn't travel in a car with me and would only go on the train. Especially when her sister who was a real mummies girl and was always at her mummies side. It probably also had something to do with the fact that my wife was also a lying bitch who I was supposed to have trusted with my deepest secrets. That is another thing that gets to you after the initial pain soothes, that your one confidant, the true love of your life, your soul mate has turned on you and treated you like shit. That doesn't go down to well either I can tell you.

I remember questioning her about the trip, she snapped well look if you don't believe me just call my Mum and she will tell you, or you can call Footlights and they will tell you that we have booked tickets with them. Of course she knew damn well that there was no way on earth that I was going to call her Mother, thinking back I should have jumped up straight away and started to dial her Mums house and waited for her reaction, well that's easy to say now as I know what it would have been, yet at the time I just accepted it because I wanted to believe it and knew that I had to accept it so that she would maybe stay over the night so that we could be together and it would all be back to normal for a night, and I liked that. It felt good, warm and cosy.

How Fucking stupid was I?

Its funny how being in love with someone, who clearly isn't in love with you makes you react to any thing that they throw at you. They could probably throw knives or shit at you and you would laugh and tell them how wonderful they are. It is sad really and I hope that one day someone will invent a drug that you can take when things like break-ups happen so that you don't become this yes person who would kiss the feet of the person who hurt them to get back with them. Anyway the thoughts were slightly clouded because at the same time my Aunty was being thrown a surprise party in Poole so at least I had something to do and take my mind of everything for a while. I went down with my daughter and my sister and her two children and we were to meet my brother and his family there.

The Party was a great bash and everybody had a great time, it was kind of sweet really because nobody asked me where my wife was. Thinking about it they had probably all be told on the great family grapevine, these are the times when these are of good use. My Daughter loved the attention that she was getting and had a wonderful evening playing with all of her cousins. She looked so happy and everybody wanted to take her home. There is such a special feeling inside when your own child holds on to you tightly when others playfully pretend that they are going to take them away, it just makes you feel so very special.

Eventually my Daughter tired out and fell asleep in her buggy so I went for a walk along the seafront late at night. I called my wife and left a few messages but she didn't call that pissed me off because I wanted to hear her voice. There was I a 6ft 2inch 16 stone guy who really needed to her a woman's voice to make me feel strong and ok with the world. I went back to the party but started to feel sad, seeing everyone else happy and laughing in couples, kissing and dancing together. There was never much time that went by where I didn't feel sad, a humorous moment would happen and I'd be enjoying myself but then something would spoil it and remind me of the fact that my wife had left me and that she had been shagging somebody else behind my back probably. Why does that happen, what had I ever done to anyone that was that bad so that I would receive a punishment like this.

Eventually when we were back in the Hotel and I carried my daughter to bed and she snuggled up into my side and was snoring away in that lovely baby snoring noise that just makes you want to sleep.

Just before I nodded off I called my wife and she answered the phone. We chatted only for a while and it seemed as if she was agitated by something then she said that she was tired and should go. I remember one of her family knocking on her door and saying goodnight you two, then realised that they meant my wife and her sister, as she told me they were sharing a room together!

That line stuck with me until I fell asleep. I just had a horrible feeling.

I remember shopping in the town on the Sunday and searching for ages for a present that I could bye for my wife from my daughter. We took ages and I looked carefully, it had to be nice, not tacky. I'm sure that she would like it no matter what it was. It ended up being a ornament for the bathroom I think, she liked ornaments. Just as we had finished shopping the phone rang and it was my wife, she was in good spirits and seemed very happy. They were just leaving Scotland on the train and she said that she couldn't wait to get home to see our daughter and that she had missed her very much. Thanks I thought what about me...still it was early days. She seemed very happy, so we said our goodbyes and I felt in a good mood and it probably showed.

We drove back and I got home quickly so that I could see my wife and chat all about the weekend. We chatted for a while and she wanted to go and give our daughter a bath, and I had to iron a shirt for the next morning.

Here We Go!

Whilst ironing I can remember seeing her handbag on the table with a handwritten letter sticking out of it. I could see that it was my wife's handwriting but it was on its side so I twisted my head to try and read it. But a voice inside told me not to as it wasn't for me and that it was wrong to do so. It was taking such will power not to read it and it was killing me to know who it was too. No I thought and I carried on ironing. My eyes kept flipping to the bag and zooming in on the letter trying to read it with my head turned sideways. No stop it I told myself, if it were for you she would have given it to you. So I finished my shirt and put away the ironing board. With that my wife appeared with our daughter, they were just getting ready for a bath.

"Can you come and take over in a minute so that I can have a bath?" my wife asked

"Of course, just give us a shout," I said and with a very jolly step she went upstairs.

I flipped through the T.V. for a while and then decided to go upstairs and get ready for my bath. As I walked into the bedroom, there was my wives handbag right in the middle of the floor and I could see that the letter was still in it. I looked at the bag and the letter and thought, ok something is telling me to read that letter, so I half closed the door, making sure that my wife wasn't coming and sat on the bed near the light, and took the letter out of the bag and unfolded it tilting it under the bedside lamp to read it.

It was one of those rare moments when you read a line and yet have to read it four or five times over so that you can actually register what you have just read and that you didn't just imagine it or dream what you read. I don't think that for the rest of my life that I will ever forget what that first sentence had said in that letter.

"I have decided to give it a go with Jo!"

I can remember thinking, hang on this doesn't make sense Jo is her friend from Oxford, what is she on about. That is why I had to read it at least Four times before the penny finally dropped inside my head.

Finally…I had found the bottom and that there was no fucking way out of this shitty mess, and that it just got as bad as it was ever going to get.

I was numb and my brain wouldn't work, what does this all mean, my head was hurting, spinning around, I could hear my heart beating faster inside, people say that as a good description of feelings and you can imaging your own heart racing pounding, but when it happened to you for real, its as if the whole world just got put on slow speed.

I scanned the letter, seeing things like," He really loves my daughter and me! I know that my husband loves me but I wish that he would just FUCKOFF sometimes and leave me alone" My eyes wouldn't scan the letter fast enough or maybe they were protecting me because to this day those are about the only things that I can remember in that whole letter, and the fact that it was to her brother who lives abroad.

I sat on the bed wondering what to say, again in complete shock, my wife was calling form the bathroom for me to go and take my daughter off her so that she could have her bath, SHIT SHIT SHIT, what am I going to do?

I thought well she is here now maybe she had changed her mind, I looked at the date on the letter it was December 31 1999. How ironic I thought New Years Fucking Eve. So I could either explode and confront her, or pretend that I had never seen the fucking thing and now that she was here she must have changed her mind. Yes I'll do that I will just forget that I had seen it atall and leave it, after all she is here now. So I walked down the hall towards the bathroom, and can remember hearing my daughter's happy laugh as she was splashing around in the bath not wanting to get out.

My wife looked at me with a big smile laughing at our daughter and said

"OOOOhhh look here's Daddy to get you out quick come on…" She smiled at me and paused, her smile half dropped and she looked very scared all in a matter of half a second and just looked at me and said "What's wrong?".

The Truth

We don't always need to know the truth, or do we? We always have this little niggle down inside our stomach sometimes and at the back of our head where we know the truth but don't want to accept it. It's like you'd rather not know the answer so you don't ask the question because you convince yourself that you know the answer, yet continue to fool yourself by denying yourself the truth.

All the times when I had thought that my wife was seeing somebody else and the millions of times that she swore that she wasn't, and I believed her like a stupid arse that I was. Now I had been handed the truth...............

But what do I do? I try and kid myself that it doesn't matter and that I will pretend that I hadn't seen it. Well now that she is here she must have made a choice between us and chosen me. Why should I rock the boat now, I have just got what I wanted she is back and I am the happiest man in the World, here we all are back under one roof and playing happy families again…God I had wanted this for so long.

"What the Fucking hell am I saying". I must be going mad, this now proves every little thing that I had ever suspected, all of the times that I was fooled by her into not believing that she wasn't seeing anyone have all just become reality in a few fucking words in a letter. I can tell you that the short walk down my hall form my bedroom to my bathroom was the longest bloody walk that I have ever had to tread. This is where you need some stupid quote like "you only know a man when you have walked a mile in his shoes"!!! A mile fucking hell I walked maybe ten paces down my hall and it nearly fucking killed me….

What the Fuck was I going to do…. I wanted to kill her, I hated her, what a bitch, she's been shagging somebody else, the dirty fucking bitch…how can I look at her…..

Then I heard her little miss I'm so sweet and lovely fucking voice….

"What's Wrong?"

"Nothing, I'm fine!" I said trying to appear as happy as I was less than 5 minutes ago.

"Come on something's wrong?"
"Honestly, nothing is wrong"
"Look there is something wrong wha...."

Before she could finish I said,

"I just read your letter..."
"What Lett..." she didn't have to finish her sentence, because she knew very fucking well which letter I thought....

With that she put her head down and burst into tears...

Good you bitch I thought, go on cry and I hope that It really fucking hurts...
But hang on who was I kidding, she wasn't hurting, its just that she had realised that she has been found out, and it only took a year.

I ignored her and then had to ask...

"So how long have you been seeing Jo?" through her tears she muttered that it had only been going on for about a month or so....

A month or so...oh that's not so bad I thought....Oh come on who was she fucking trying to kid, she had written that she wanted to give it a go with fuckwit Jo, what was I doing almost believing her again....

"Oh come on you must think that I was born fucking yesterday…"I was trying to keep as calm as I could because our daughter was wondering about with her towel on.

"Look we talked at first and just became friends, but it had been two months maximum!"

"Did you have sex" God that was a very hard question, but I thought whilst I was here in hell I might just as well get all of the gory shitty details that there was to find out!

The answer seemed to take a lifetime to come out…(Please be no I was thinking, please be no….)

"Yes…but the thing is that we…"

"But you nothing" I shouted.

I felt as though I was watching a film, and that things had slowed down. I still couldn't register what I had just learnt. My wife has been having sex with somebody else, whilst married to me, behind my back and…..then I was bought back to normality by my daughter laughing and pulling at my hand.

I had to get out of the house… because a crime of passion was about to happen if I had stayed… I never have and never will hit a woman, but thought that if ever there was a time when I should have wanted to it should be now, but I just felt dirty and disgusted, I'd been sleeping in a bed with my wife, being kind loving patient, caring about her situation and all the time realising now that the BITCH was shagging some other bloke,

"Wait….you cant just go off……Look lets talk about this ….please we need to talk…"

With that I slammed the front door and left. I remember that it was pissing down with rain, and all that I had on was a tee shirt and a pair of jogging bottoms and my slipper, yes I know how sad I wear slippers…..!

I had the letter in my hand and tried to stop myself reading it…I would lift it up then put it down, then try again, each time getting nearer to reading it but then decided that look my life really has hit the bottom, my wife has left me, come back left again, swore on my daughters life that she was not seeing anyone, moved back in again and then I find a letter to her brother that explains she is going to give it a go with the fuck-wit that she had been shagging for the last two months(she said)…….This doesn't make scene….

So I read on…. I'd get through a couple of lines and then get to a bit which talked about then, and how much he loved her and my daughter, and how she knew that I loved her but she wished that I would just.. "FUCKOFF" and leave her alone… It was kind of like when you see somebody read a letter in a film and they obviously get to a bit that they don't like as I had just did and then they go into their overacting bit and throw there arms in the air and kick something like a bin or a wall or car… Well I now know how very good that those actors are, because it is exactly what happens when you read a letter this painful.

Onlookers must have thought that one of those Looney tunes had escaped from the funny farm, I can imagine them explaining to the policeman, "Yes he is a large man in a tee shirt and jogging bottoms with slippers on and no socks, soaked through to the bone and shouting and kicking bins, he appears a little upset....

A little upset well that was a fucking underestimation....it is unbelievably hard for me to actually try and remember how I felt... but nothing else in the world matters....everything bad that could happen to you in a lifetime all put together couldn't be this bad. The crushing pain feeling in your heart is devastating.... even worse was the fact that I knew I had to go back and face her and the last thing in the world that I wanted to do was go back to that house and face her.

Why???

They say that all things in life are sent to try us... Well I can tell you this certainly tried me to the point of where i nearly gave up on everything. I wouldn't wish that pain on anyone, but the fact is that it happens everyday. I know that sometimes people finish relationships and both of them agree, and sometimes one of them is a little upset or even both, but I think that for the majority of relationships that end that one person is destroyed. That feeling of complete uselessness is so hard top come to terms with, and everybody tells you that you have to learn to live with it, you know that you do and only hope that some day that you will but at that moment in your life you feel that the pain and hurt will never end, and it is the worst thing in the world that has ever happened as far as you are concerned.

The truth is that it will one day become a lesser pain, but it will remain with you for the rest of your life.

Afterall it's a pretty big think when your one true love of your life suddenly leaves you, and when children are involved that is when it hurts twice as much. Still at the end of the day if she wants to leave you then there is absolutely nothing that you can do. Beg steal borrow, hang on to her legs, nothing will stop her if she wants to go, and take your children too. That is just so fucked up and so unfair.

So the only thing that you can do is just hope that you get over the initial pain quickly and then let the rot set in of future pain for wanting them to come back to you. I remember her calling me as I left, crying and her shaking voice, "Look please lets talk about it." Oh Die you bitch is all that I remember thinking. But knew that I had to go back some time so I made my way back to the house. The worst thing was I couldn't just sneak in and go and hide because in my haste I had left without a key so had to get her to let me in. I couldn't even look at her and just walked straight past her into the dinning room. Luckily my daughter had gone to bed. I sat in the dark and just really had a blank mind. I know now that I was in shock and trying to understand what this now meant, but my mind had just closed shut down. I'd eventually had enough. I didn't want to give up but there was nothing left inside of me to fight with.

"Look we need to talk about this and try to put it behind us...it's been over for a while and it was just a bit a fun and I have been stupid. I never really liked him and knew that it would never work, but things just happened, it wasn't planned..."

I could hear my wife talking and was only really catching the odd words hear and there...it was as if somebody was talking through a wall when it all sounds muffled. I must have sat there for a couple of hours and then realised that she wasn't there anymore talking. I hope that she might have left the house, but she was in the other room. I still couldn't look at her.

"Why?" was all I said.

"It just happened."

"Why?"

"Look it was stupid, I was stupid I admit, but look it's over now and I'm back here with you trying to make it work!"

"I can't carry on now knowing that you have been shagging someone else, it will never be the same, do you honestly think that I could take you back now. You know that I couldn't do that, ever...

"But why? Look its was just a stupid fling that meant nothing, we have only really spent a couple of weeks together if you add up all of the time....it was over as soon as it began really......!

He's nothing like you, and we don't even get on, he's thick as a tree and we don't even have anything in common. I don't enjoy anything with him.

"Just sex then was it, you obviously have enough in common to fuck him don't you…you…" I wanted to scream you FUCKING COW…but stopped myself.

It was a weird concept, I was looking at this woman on the other side of the room sat there now with no real emotion telling me that she had an affair with someone, but it didn't mean anything, that he was thick and stupid etc… and she wanted to come back and make it work, it will be ok etc…etc… and I realised hang on a minute…i don't know you…who are you. That threw me and I think I realised I didn't know her.

It went round and round in my heard yet I just wouldn't understand why. I kept asking her to explain to me why, but she couldn't. I started to delve within the banks of my memory about all the times when I had suspected something wrong. She of course denied any of them. I can remember thinking that I still did not want to believe this and that I can get over it and that everything would work itself out and we would be ok. Who was I kidding though? Yet people split up and get back together all of the time don't they, I can do it, why should I be so special as to not handle it. It's amazing how you think when threatened with something you now is going to hurt you.

She eventually went to bed after I had just gone blank. I felt such a sense of relief when she had gone to bed, I could now finally relax without her in the room. That was probably a mistake and I just began to cry.

The difference is this time I knew the truth that I had feared for the last year. I had cried before many a time and it always hurt. But this time it was a different hurt. I had a definite reason to cry this time. Whereas before I used to tell myself to pull myself together, and that she would soon be back.........Now I knew the truth and that it was never going to be the same again, I now knew that she had been with someone else, and then the self torture starts, you try to blank it out but have visions of them together, him as she described him a short fat bald man and her rolling about in bed naked kissing etc etc...... and I just ended up worse off and beating myself up about it.

Eventually I must have drifted off but it was late into the night. I can remember the first think to be disrupted after the initial shock of her leaving was my sleeping patterns and then my eating habits. Oh well I thought that I could do with loosing a few pounds again...i mean I'd become a bit happier with the prospect of us being back together...typical. I would ask God the question over and over...."What have I done...when did I do it? Was I really that much of a bastard to deserve this punishment from him?"

The thing is that I had not done anything....

From that point my wife and I talked every night after my daughter had gone to bed, we went over everything. I was trying to find out if she still loved me and wanted this thing to work again. But on the other had was not sure if that is exactly what I wanted. I was petrified of loosing my family. I knew that if it didn't work that she would be off again and that would blow any chance of us getting back together. I was in such a shit way... I think back now and really do wonder how I got through it all to this day. So what do I do?

After thinking about we discussed it and left it that we would just see how we got on. Try it and "Go with the flow".....

It was ok for a while, but I remember that it wasn't me. I knew that I was trying to hard and making sure that everyone was happy all of the time.... Making tea...doing more that my fair share of everything and generally being over the top. I just decided that I wanted it to work and wanted this to be ok.

Results.

Time is a great healer was probably one of my favourite little pep talks that I would give myself. Things were ok between us but it was obvious to me that we were certainly skating on the thin ice part of life…

My wife and I were sleeping in the same bed together as before but nothing sexual was going on. I can remember after she had been back for a bout a week I asked if we were ever going to kiss? We laughed a little and then said that we would try one…it was like kissing a dead fish…(I imagine..)

Oh well there' time I thought, plenty of time. My wife insisted that she did still love me and that the Sexual side was something that would eventually come back. Once we have done it once then it will be fine she said…(Fat chance I thought.) I just found it very weird that usually the first thing about a couple's relationship is the sexual side. The animal attraction between two humans was there is the first instance…but for us it just wasn't there for her. I certainly still fancied her and indeed still deep down loved her and wanted that sexual side back, it was just time she said. Had I been here before or was this déjà vu? I just didn't know anymore, I don't think that I really cared anyway.

After approximately two weeks I can remember jumping out of bed at about two o'clock in the morning and telling her that I had just had enough it was not going to work and that I wanted a divorce, I was calm and just said it as simply as that …"I want a divorce".

My wife started to panic and cry…

"But what about our daughter? What will we do….It will upset her! Can't we try going to counselling and talking to somebody to help us through it?"

It was weird that now the tables had turned, whereas now it was her that was crying and reflecting on what was about to happen. I thought good now you know how It fucking feels, and hope you feel like shit. She was crying and panicking about the prospects. But I couldn't give a shit.

I said that I needed a break and that I was going to go away that weekend to think about things.

Later on in the week my wife agreed that it would be good for me to have some time alone, and said that she was going to go and see her friend in Oxford who we had all recently visited. I remember vividly that morning because her car battery was flat and I took it with her to get it fixed. The Bitch never even said thank you.

So I went off somewhere just to get away from everything. It was hard to imagine life forever without my wife. We had become best friends before all of this. I couldn't reach a decision after thinking all weekend so decided to leave it go on as it was at the moment and just see if we could possibly get back as we were.

Bitch Form Hell!!!

I got back early on the Sunday as my wife said that she would be back in the afternoon. I got the chance to have a good think about all of the shit that had been going on in the past year or so, and had made up my mind to give it a bloody good go for all of our sakes.

"Let's face it mate, neither of you were virgins when you met each other…"

One of my closest friends told me that once when I was having doubts about my wife, when I had found out she cheated on a former boyfriend with his brother and it bothered me. In someway now he still says that it was his fault that we got married because he changed my mind about her…yes your right it is all your fault.(Just kidding Mr.T.)

David Simpson

I must have nodded off and heard the car door slam outside and the front door opening; I heard my wife calling and went out to see them. I was so happy to see my daughter smiling away at me and I took her into the front room. I became puzzled though because I could smell a familiar smell on her skin whilst I gave her a cuddle.

"She smells Funny" I said to my wife…

"let me smell…..Oh that's Tanya's new perfume….i didn't like it."

"That smell's like aftershave to me…" My heart was now beating faster and I was angry, that was aftershave…had she? could she have.

"Don't be stupid she said…"

I walked into the kitchen holding my daughter, talking away to her asking her if she wanted any food, she was just being a gorgeous baby and making noises and trying to smile back.

Then my wife came in behind us and was saying that she was going to make a tea and did I want one?

As I turned to answer her, I noticed that her face was all red.

"Was it sunny today in Oxford?"I asked?

"No why?"

"Because you're whole face is very red…"

"Oh y-y-yeah…. that was the um s-sofa bed that Tanya has got that I slept on it has um v-very rough material…"

With that I just looked at her…i knew damn bloody well what it was, she has very sensitive skin and I can remember what happened to her when I didn't shave.

"How fucking stupid do you think I am?…I said through gritted teeth.

"You dirty bitch…"

I walked off into the front room…. she followed me. I put my daughter down on her play blanket and left the room. My wife was pretending to look upset and shocked and said that she hadn't been anywhere near, "The thick fat bastard" she protested.

I went into the Kitchen hoping again to myself that maybe I had made a mistake and she was telling the truth. That's what I wanted to have happened, but this time I knew that I was not wrong.

So I had to prove it to myself. I looked into her handbag for any signs of clues. I found a ticket for a Parkside wildlife park in Broxbourne, Hertfordshire, it had today's date on the receipt. I put it back and went into the front room.

"So where did you go today with Tanya then?"

"To the same wildlife park that we went to in Oxford a few weeks back when we all went down."

"So what were you doing at the Parkside wildlife park? She went quite and shocked and eventually asked me,

"How did you know that I was in Broxbourne..?"

"I didn't, you just told me………." I felt a rage now unlike any I had felt before….it was a different kind of pain because I knew right then that it was definitely over for ever.

"you were with that fucking fat bald thick wanker Jo weren't you…..

"With tears running down her face she agreed…"

"Get out you filthy dirty bitch."

"W-w-w-what….W-w-where am I supposed to go? You can't just throw me out on the streets."

"Go now get out" I screamed.

"I'll have to come back tomorrow."

"Just get out." I couldn't believe that it was all finally over.

"Can't we talk about this we must be able to…."

"Get out."

She picked up her bag, faked a tearful exit and stood at the front door. She stood there for quite a while, and I have always wondered weather she was thinking, god what have I done, or now I have to leave?

To be honest with you I don't really care what she was feeling I was just glad when I heard that door slam and her drive away.

Then I sat after my daughter was asleep and broke down.

You then realise that you have been living on a prayer for so very long and know that when you have been fearing something for so long, you still have that little bit of hope inside that keeps you alive by telling you that, hey maybe it will all be ok soon. That's what keeps you getting up in the morning, and occasionally being able to enjoy yourself one little tiny thought that this might all be ok one day. People ask you how everything is, you still tell people that you and the wife are having a few problems but things are looking a bit better, she just needed some time to herself.

Again that little white light that you have created yourself keeps you in there.........

The Problem then is what happens when you realise that it is all over. A tiny voice is already saying, look so things cannot get any worse now just start from here there can be no more bad news...but then I think for once it is time for you to admit to yourself that that's it, I had been fooling myself for a year now and wasted all of that time in the hope that she would have come back. I remember sitting they're thinking how exhausted I was, it really had been a long time a very long time but I had got there. I should have listened to my Dad when he said that

"Look if she was going to have come back she would have done by now, you have to get on with your own life, move on."

That was 6 months ago, but that's life. It does take a lot to admit defeat............then you realise just how vulnerable that we all are, its not something that you usually think about, or if you're the person that does the leaving, it doesn't bother you then, I mean how many times have we all dumped somebody and ever thought about their feelings. I mean sure we think for a couple of minutes of how bad or upset that they are going to be but we don't ever take time to reflect how this is going to effect them, why should we its not us that are upset, we just want to get out of the relationship as fast as we can. It's a very lonely place when it does finally happen to us. You feel very alone, and no one can help us. The truth is they can help by talking to us, but at the time, it's not an option, you feel stupid betrayed let down and destroyed.

What Next?

What the hell do I do now? I can look back many many times and i have, I tried to remember if there was some magic formula that I found to help me get on. To tell the truth there wasn't one and to this day you never really get it out of your system. All that happens is you learn to accept the result. So this was my new start, she had made her decision and I had to act accordingly. In some ways that is the worst thing, SHE had made the decision and I had no say in it atall. You never realise it when you finish with someone, but that is a major problem we on the dumped side have to accept the decision and there is fuck all that we can do about it. It's a kick in the balls but that is how it is. So life…and getting on with it day by day had to be the way forward look for me.

The I realised that this nightmare was still in motion because my wife had moved back in with me…the new start the new beginning, Well it was that alright but I had to now endure her staying in my house knowing that she had been sneaking off all of the time and shagging that arsehole bread man.

What a bitch!!!! You try and block out the thoughts of them together, trying to imagine what he looks like, what they did, where they went, all of those things but its like a devil that keeps reminding you of what went on. I tried to do something to occupy my time so that I didn't think about it, but no matter what you do those horrible thoughts come through and niggled away.

I even thought about the fact that she probably left the house and went straight back to him who she had just spent the weekend with. The lies that she told me. I pictured in my head all of the times when I had asked her if there was anybody else and she had sworn that there wasn't. The times that she went out, everything that I had been paranoid about now turns out that I was right to be suspicious, how stupid did I feel now. She had even sworn on our daughter's life twice that she wasn't seeing anyone!

She returned home the next day sheepishly and didn't say much. I couldn't believe that she had the guts to turn up and stay in my house. Why didn't she go off as she did before and stay with a friend. Why should I have her under my roof? Looking at it now, maybe everyone had turned there back on her because they had maybe warned her that this would one day happen and that it would all blow up in her face. I told her once I found out about him "Look tell me everything now because one day this will all come out, the whole truth will show itself and make it worse for you!"

"I have told you everything, everything!"

She was lying. I could tell.

The thing was as much as I wanted to believe her I could tell that there was more, and I was going to find out. Why? God knows maybe it was that stupid old thing called PRIDE again. Surely it couldn't be good but I just had to know. Why would you want to know more hurt? I suppose just in case it came out years later, once and for all I had put it all behind me.

Luckily for me we had all planned to go on Holiday the following week to Spain, for sure that was now going to change I was still going as I had to get away form all of this, so I told my wife that I was still going with our daughter but she wasn't allowed to come, and that by the time I came back I wanted her gone and out of my house.

"I haven't got any money, I can't afford it!" She screamed.

"Tough shit, go and life with fuck nuts..." I said.

"you just haven't listened have you. Were not together in that way anymore, were just friends.!"

"Oh yeah, and I go around and shag all of my friends don't i. And I suppose your still going to tell me that you promise me that you had only been seeing him for two months…"

She walked off. I followed her and gave her a solution to her problem. I will give you enough money to get out, I'll give you the deposit and you can just go.

I hated her and everything about her, but at the same time still loved her, fuck knows why after what she had done to me in the past year. So the time came nearer for my holiday and I just couldn't wait for it. The feelings of hurt are a strange one…. total numbness inside…and such immense anger. I had thought about going to his work, as it was the same company as hers and walking in and kicking the fucking crap out of him! But in the end yes I would have felt a bit better but was it his fault? As far as he was aware she was single and living on her own. I very nearly did it a couple of times but eventually realised that it would do no good, and I'd probably get an assault charge and have to pay him money…! That would be good wouldn't it, id have to pay the man compensation, the man who has now my wife. "Fucking Tosser." Yet we all know that one day this will all come back on him, what goes around comes around Mr Bread Man….

The next day I took my daughter to the childminders. They were all outside in the back garden and I spoke to the childminders daughter who was a friend of ours. She could tell that something was very wrong, and I started to talk and I think it just all poured out, my anger my hate, everything. She just looked at me with tears in her eyes and said that she was so sorry. Then the childminder said, "We told her not to be so stupid, her and that bloke, how ridiculous it all was and what she was going to lose". I turned to our friend and said,

"How long was it going on for?"
"Well she told me that it was since about June, but things she said make me think that it was longer than that.!"

Instantly she knew that she had just told me the wrong thing.

"What is it?" She asked.

I started to fill up with tears but managed to hold them back. I took a deep breath and thought for a minute.
"The thing is that she told me they started to become Friends in November, but I think that you have just confirmed my thoughts that it was longer than she told me."
"Oh God I'm so sorry I…."
I didn't let her finish as I said goodbye and left…she looked horrified, and knew that she had just let me know another part of the untold story.

More shit…. how much more shit is there I wondered. I stopped and thought for a moment though, maybe I should just let all of this shit go. Why was I hanging on to it all? She has left me, had an affair, deceived me, committed adultery, lied to everyone we knew shouldn't I just leave it now and try to rebuild my life?

Bollocks I thought to myself, I want her to know that I knew she had been lying to me again the little cow. So I called my wife at work and told her to meet me at home NOW.

"Why" She asked innocently, so I told her that I had just found out that she had been seeing that Wanker for a lot longer that she had told me. The phone went very quiet and she finally agreed to meet me.

I didn't know what I was going to say, or why I asked her to meet me, I had no plan, I think that I just wanted to shout at her to let her know how pissed off I was and to let out a bit of anger. I got to the house and sat in the kitchen and waited. I remember my pulse starting to race and I heard the beep beep of her alarm. She came into the house and stood there and said nothing.

"Why the fuck did you tell me that it was only since November that you were seeing him, when all the time it was more like the November last year. Why have you just lied and lied again and again. Do you know how to tell the fucking truth?" I was loosing my temper big time and knew it but for once I didn't care, I couldn't make it any worse. I kicked the cupboard and shouted again, "Why didn't you just come clean a year ago, told the truth and then I wouldn't have wasted a fucking year off my life on waiting around for you. All the help I tried to give you, calling Doctors, Midwifes, and Councillors why the fuck didn't you just tell me to FUCKOFF and had done with it. Why let me make a complete arse of myself for the past years chasing around after you.!" She said nothing and just sat at the table.

"Tell me something…were you seeing dickhead before you left me?" She sat there and started to cry.

"Don't start that bollocks again because this time it wont work, DID YOU LEAVE ME FOR HIM!"

"This is typical of you…You're so planned and have to know everything, that's the problem with you!" she screamed.

"Oh fuck well I'm so sorry, the fact that I want to know if my wife has been fucking someone else whilst pretending to be the dutiful wife, sorry for being so nosey." She really had me pissed off now.

"Look I'm going back to work." Then she left and slammed the door.

I just sat there for a while to contemplate the world and what was I going to do now. Again I felt so lonely. But what was new, it was a place that I was getting to now quite well; I felt as if I had a permanent place there, my own seat kept warm.

So the following day I gave my wife a bankers draft for the rent and deposit and felt safe in the knowledge that she would be gone by the time that I got back. I asked her just one favour before I left and I think the only one that I asked of her, "No matter what please do not have that wanker anywhere near my house, no matter what. Despite her standing there and promising me that she wouldn't I found out later that he was there and helped her move out of the house? He may have even stayed the night and shagged her in my house in one of my beds... After all that she had done to me, she couldn't even do that.

I left for holiday the next morning with my daughter and my Father!

The Pain In Spain!

It was nice to get far away from home and all of the shit that went with it. There is something cleansing in travel, it really is like leaving all of your troubles behind you. You fall into this false sense of security and enter this numb world where everything seems ok. I guess that is why we go on holidays to forget, the problem is we know that it is still all there when we get back home. Watching my daughter playing in the sand on the beech I was so happy just to be with her, I would have loved to of stayed in Spain and never have to go back, but I knew that wasn't an option. I knew that now the real horrible shit would have to begin, life apart from my daughter was the biggest problem for me. You become much engrossed with the constant forming child in front of you every hour of every day, it takes over you life instantly but you don't care, it is something that to me was a wonderful experience, but I knew that this was going to change now and I would become a "Part Time" Dad. I know that people say oh don't be so silly she will always know who her Daddy is, but that isn't the point, I had to deal with the fact that some Fucking Wanker was shagging my Wife and seeing more of my Daughter than I was and that is what cut me up inside more now.

It was as if everything shifted in priority, I had no feelings at the moment for my wife except absolute hate. I wished that she would get hurt by this new feller she had and that he would cause her a huge upset that would cripple her as emotionally as she had done to me. Not a very Christian was of thinking some might say but the way that I saw it was, what had God or Christianity done for me lately? Bugger all except destroy my family life forever. You see I had found the perfect time and place in my life and it was exactly where I wanted to be. I had a beautiful loving wife, and then a even more beautiful gift my very own flesh and blood, my little "Baby Girl" she made everything in my life 100% Complete and I never took that for granted. The warmth inside when you have all you need is such a settling feeling, one of indescribable comparison to anything that you have ever had before. You know that in a while you could hopefully extend this pleasure with more children as we had planned to and create a unit that nothing could intentionally destroy.

Children can make and break your heart in a matter of a second just by saying something or accidentally hurting themselves, it is a strong hold that they have on you, and how hard your strive to ensure that nothing will ever harm them, and where as before things in life, small things sometime were a chore or strain, have now all changed and you know that if you had to you would move mountains, Kill or even die before you let anything happen to your own child. I think that they also change the way you feel about others, they come first before anything else.

I believe that is a natural progression though and it is a sacrifice that everyone in the world makes and nobody dare question. Your children are first and for me that is a natural choice and I'm sure it is for nearly everyone else. I watch my daughter intently and just cant believe what happens in life, the way that she changes and grows and how fast it all happens, and how at her age she doesn't have a care in the world.

We have an amazing bond between us and I know that as she grows so will the bond. I know perfectly well that there will be difficult times ahead as she gets older but that is how we all change and adapt, with age comes knowledge. The only problem is that when your sixteen you think that you know everything. I know at that age I did. You are exploring the boundaries of life at sixteen although you believe you are winning the game. Teenagers will always be difficult. I was just one who thought he knew it all, I didn't get into much trouble just went slightly off the rails. I remember not getting on with my Dad and leaving home. I moved up North and lived with my sister.

My Father has always been hard and strict, not very emotional and I wanted to get away. The thing is though that time in you life is the model for the future you. What you do everyday has a development in the rest of your life. You could be self-motivated, hard working but I think that the most important thing is to be proud. If you take pride in everything you do then no one has any reason ever to complain. If you put 100% of your effort and time into each task then your going to get the best result out of it. We have all done something in our lives where we must have said to ourselves on completion, 'hey now that's ok but could be better,' when in reality we now that its pretty bad and know damn well that it could be much better, so we make ourselves re-do it and this time complete the task to the very best of our ability then we feel much better. Our standards are all different though, but that's what makes us all different. The same happens in life. If we mess up then we should learn from that mistake and next time we know. I learnt while I was away that all my Father was doing when he was strict was modelling me for the future.

We don't understand it at the time and want to know why our parents are being so difficult when in reality they are just trying to teach us that life isn't all playing in the garden and joking around, life is also serious where pretty bad things can also happen.

But thankfully I realised that my Father was trying to prepare me for the world and what I had to do. It must have worked because now when I do things I think if it's to my best ability and if he would think so. I guess we all want our parents to think that we have done them proud. It seems that Men seek approval form their Father and Women the Mothers. I suppose the Mother gets a rough deal from the Sons sometimes but they know that we love them really. The only problem is though that to our parents we are always children. For the rest of our lives they are the teacher and we are the student. Even now at my tender age of 31 my father still makes me feel about ten years old when explaining something to me. I am guessing that this feeling will never go away and even when I'm fifty he will still make me feel ten. Yet the one good thing that you can always rely on is that they will be there.

The holiday that we embarked on must have been difficult time for my Father, to know how to discuss with your son the pain and troubles in his life. As bad luck would have it though I think he was getting the hang of it as I was the youngest of four and was the fourth to go through a divorce. However we all have different reactions to emotional pain so I suppose you never know what to expect but I bet he could probably just repeat what he had said the other three times. He must think that his children are jinxed.

Going back to the pride thing though, In all of the time that this was going on in my life I wanted my

Father to think that I could handle this, to be a man be strong and had bared up quite well when ever he talked to me about it. In true parental style though they leave it up to you to initiate the conversation because I think they fear what reaction it might have if they bring it up, anger, tears, a real Pandora's box, so they wait for you .

The most poignant time that I remember was New Years Eve. I was getting ready to go out at my parents. I was going to a party and was quite happy trying to forget the recent events. I was in the middle of showering and suddenly felt upset. It's a horrible emotion that all of a sudden grabs you when your not expecting it. From out of nowhere you go from perfectly happy to desperately sad. I just stood there for a minute and tried to fight it off. It's like something trying to get out, a feeling of pressure from inside building and building up.

The shower had gone cold and I hadn't realised yet but it diverted my attention and I felt ok again. Thank God for that it had passed. I continued to get ready and went down stairs. At the bottom of the stairs the feeling returned. This time is was worse. My stomach was in a knot and the pressure inside was immense. I knew I was about to burst into tears but again tried to hold it in. I stood in the hallway at my parents pacing from foot to foot hoping that the feeling would pass again. It wasn't going anywhere though. I could hear my Mums TV on and also my Dad's.

What should I do? God I wish this would all just go away. The pressure inside was building and my stomach was hurting. It hadn't been this bad for along time. I was now in the kitchen and could see my Dads feet sticking out from behind the door. I wanted him to make it alright, why doesn't he know what to do. I thought about going in to talk to him but knew that I wouldn't get any words out. No I cant go in there I will just be a mess of tears and pain. I paced the kitchen and kept trying to suppress the feeling and hope it would go away, but all I could think about was my Dad. Why hadn't he come out to see me?

Surely he knew I was in pain. I paced the kitchen the other way and decided to talk with him. I walked into the room and looked at him all I wanted was a cuddle.

I think it reverts to the times in your childhood when you want to feel safe and know that in your parents arms you were completely safe, nothing could harm you in those arms, and I'm sure that remains with you forever.

We have all seen it on TV when there is a Mum or a Dad hugging a crying son or daughter and we just think god get a grip you wuss, but we soon all dive for cover into those arms again when we need reassurance or comfort, just to hear those words again, "It will be ok" and it does.

I think that there is just a natural instinct then for parents that take over and I just felt those huge arms and hands around me and I just let it all go. It was if I was crying for the first time since all of this had happened. Nothing was said, and nothing needed to be said, the gentle rocking and tight squeezing around me were words enough. I just stayed there and wanted to stay there forever until everything was gone away. It is a wonderful feeling. One that can only be described by grabbing hold of a parent when you are in such pain. All I heard was my Fathers words over and over again.

"If I could do anything then you know that I would."

I don't know why I suddenly remembered that, it is now something that I felt embarrassed about and in some ways hope that he had forgotten, but it probably helped my Father and made him feel that he was able to do something, and he should know that it did, Dad thank you for that hug it helped me more than anything you could imagine. I think that it was just sitting in their apartment watching my Father sitting there reading his book, reminded me of that night.

With Mums I think that we all naturally turn to them and my Mother was my strength, she was there every time that I turned around for her, they seem to have this power to know just when to be there for us. My Mother had lots of times to rescue me in my life through all kinds of troubles, but this was I think the worst test that I had put her through unintentionally of course but I can honestly say that Mum you were magnificent.

It must be hard for our family and friends when we are distraught in emotional pain like this, but I think that we should all allow them to be there in what ever capacity that they can because they feel just as bad watching us go through it as we do whilst we try to get through it. We know that they are all full of good advice at these times and we often ask them and our friends what they think, what would they do. Only problem is we just end up doing what we want to do, or what our feelings make us do. After all feelings are hard to control. Yet talking to friends and Family is good for us, it allows us to get things off our chest and out in the open. We also get many different opinions when we discuss it with a friend, which then allows us to see our problem from its many angles.

I used to sit and watch my daughter as she slept and trying not to think of the times that remain ahead when we wouldn't be together. I blocked it out for must of the Holiday and just enjoyed every second of every day with her, she was mine twenty-four hours a day and nothing in the world would change that nothing. We played, laughed, cuddled and just enjoyed the time together. Throughout the whole holiday my Father and I never discussed my problems. In some ways it was nice as I gave me a break from it all.

The next time that I thought about my situation was on the plane home, shit what do I do. I was set to move house, I had sold mine and put the deposit down on the new house that my wife an I were going to start again in, Jesus what a mess. We had even gone around this new house together and picked out the tiles for the Kitchen, Bathroom and carpets for the rooms, even the bloody colours of paint. She knew all the time that she was messing about with my life. How could I move into this new house now? Or would it be a new start for me? Maybe that was the way to look at it. I put it our of my head as I look ed down at my daughter asleep on my lap.

I think that it was about this time when I really understood that my marriage was well and truly over. I went over it again and again in my mind all the different scenarios that could unfold in the next phase of my life. Could it work again between us? This was the question! All through my life I have been a stubborn git in terms of forgiving people and held grudges for years, my Mum always laughs at the first time that I remember holding a grudge, I was only a young boy about 9 or 10 and we were visiting my Grandparents in Gloucester and I bought my first record, it was Heartbreak Hotel by Elvis.

I was so excited and felt so grown up with my new and only record holding it up for all of the shoppers to see. When we got back to my Grandparents house I asked my uncle if I could play my record on his stereo system and he said no! I was so upset; all I wanted to do was hear my new record. I didn't want to touch it, just hear it but he refused to put it on. My Mother told me not to worry and made some excuse. We then travelled to my Fathers Parents in Wales the next day and I asked my Other Nan if she had a record player,

"Oh yes I think I have" she said and it was on of those very old ones in a little box that had a speaker built in and had the facility to stack up the records on the top and the next one dropped down automatically when the last one had finished. It was red and had a white mesh on the front over the speaker. It was a bit wobbly and I had to stick a two pence piece on the arm so that the needle sat on the record. But as I recall Elvis had never sounded better.

For years I held this against my uncle and when I was about 22 my Mother reminded of this and how much he had upset me. He took me fishing the next time we were there and during the day he turned to me and said,

"Maybe this will make up for the time when I didn't let you play your record on my stereo!" I laughed and instantly the grudge that I had bared for all of these years was gone. I felt very stupid then but was glad that I could finally forgive him. Thanks for the days fishing Uncle M.

So could I learn to forgive and forget this with my wife? I tried but knew that it was a little more serious than her not letting me play a record. The time was drawing near to moving houses and I still thought that it would be a good fresh start in a new house for my daughter and me.

Other Women!

During the last year whilst in my depressed state I made conscious efforts to go out and stop myself form sitting in and being even more depressed. Eventually over the first 6 months or so, I was able to stop the lies about my relationship going form oh my wife is away, to we need a break and are having some time apart to eventually having the stomach to tell people that my wife had left me and I didn't have a clue as to why. Its amazing the support that friends give you too. Yet you know when you tell them the truth that they turn around and say,

'I knew that there was something wrong'.

I had as a young lad enjoyed the company of the Girls, (That's putting it politely). During these last months there were lots of women that would sit and talk to you for hours about your problems with relationships and a broken-down marriage. I can tell you it is a great chat up line men, women just love to talk to a broken man. I think that is just their mothering instinct. The fact is though women talk a lot of sense about relationships. They seem to know what to say to make you feel a bit better. I understood women a bit more during this, they are far more sensitive than us guy's and just for a while I felt ashamed about all of the women that I had upset in my previous years and relationships. Then I realised that for once in my life I was the victim.

I made very good friends with a girl that I used to know and we talked every time that I saw her when I was out. I then realised that I liked her more than I first felt. I eventually asked her out and she accepted. "What took you so long" she asked?

I didn't have to think too long about that one. All of the time that I was alone waiting for my wife to come back, there had been a few women that I liked but told couldn't date them because I thought that when I got back with my wife I would have to come clean and tell her that I had been out with somebody else. This I thought would definitely make her tell me that she couldn't be with me again as I had been with someone else. I know that is a silly way to think but its not a time for rational thinking. I mean just think back to that Yucca Plant.

But the situation makes you think these things and depending on how desperate you are you hang on to whatever dreams you can and I truly believed that if I had of had a relationship with someone else then my wife wouldn't want me. As a result of these thoughts I never in all of the time that I was waiting for my wife to come back had more that a kiss and cuddle with a woman. It was a block that was not going to go away.

Still there is no sense in looking back. I talked to them because all of a sudden it made me feel good that a woman, a very attractive woman at that could find me interesting, which made me feel better about myself and I felt wanted. I realised then that maybe all women were not all bad. Yet later on I felt guilty because I had talked to someone else and found them attractive. How stupid is that!!!

The thing was though I had a very good reason not to go any further with any kind of relationship. In the whole year that I sat waiting I only kissed two different girls. Hopefully one day if they ever read this then they will know the reasons why the relationships went no further. It wasn't because I didn't fancy you it was as above. Another time, another life who knows. Its like the one woman that we have all let go without talking too that we regret for the rest of our lives, we will never know what could have been!

So once I knew that my marriage was as good as dead and buried I asked this girl out. We had fun and she made me laugh a lot. It was a weird experience and

I still felt a little guilty about the whole thing but tried to take it a day at a time.

It was difficult because my wife and I were still taking care of out daughter alternate nights so I never could plan much in terms of a relationship, but that was the furthest thing from my mind my daughter was first and always will be. So a girlfriend of mine has to fit in around my Daughter / Daddy time, like it or not.

It turns out that this girl wanted a bit more commitment in terms of the day-by-day relationship that we had. This was awkward for me and I started to find faults with her. This I think is a natural thing that happens, I can remember thinking, God I could not marry her she just isn't right so what's the point in all of this. I would look way in to the future and decide that I just couldn't see myself with her so gave up. That is a terrible way to look at things but I guess that's what being really hurt is all about. I was putting obstacles in the way of any potential relationship in the fear that it would go bad anyway so might as well end it now. Looking back I think that I just wasn't ready for anything. I have extremely high barriers up and they are still there now. I know why they are there yet don't know how to get them down talking to a therapist might be one way yet I don't think that I can do this. Hopefully one day someone will read this and tell me exactly how to get them down.

In the relationship side of things the One thing that I was most petrified off was SEX!!!!

To me now sex was a way to make babies, which of course it is, but I got scared and just would destroy myself with the fear that if I had SEX that she would get pregnant and have a baby. I can tell you it is the best form of contraception and it is guaranteed!!! I just thought that I couldn't ever have another baby because it would some how detract my attention from my daughter and I couldn't do that.

Anyway it had been over a year since I had had SEX and it didn't bother me. We did eventually have SEX in a drunken romp and yes we did use protection as I had voiced my greatest fears of the natural result in men and women having sex. I have never been so scared afterwards as to what if!!!

I was then worried until her period, petrified of it. Luckily everything was ok. But it was a worry that I didn't need right now in my life so ended the relationship and became celibate again. At least you cant get anybody pregnant that way. So it was back to being single and living the bachelor life without the women involved. Don't get me wrong I still like women but just couldn't have a relationship with one.

Some people are able to survive on their own. I don't think that I am one of them. I get very lonely and so bored. I know that we all need time on our own, but usually five minutes is enough for me then I need to talk to someone. If there is nobody there then I just talk to myself. Its not a crazy thing, I just pass the time by having made up conversations. I know that lots of us might say something to ourselves like,

'Oh god how can you have been so stupid' when we have done something wrong. But that's different I really do have conversations about absolute crap. I also take on board the part of the other person that I am talking to. This is a thing that I have been doing for years so don't worry its not something that will happen to you if your wife has just left you.

Why do I do it? I have absolutely no idea. The good thing is though it passes the time and makes car journeys interesting. Maybe I am completely mad, but I would like to say just different.

Moving House!

Regarding my moving to my new house, new start the time had now come to "Tie In" as the solicitor told me. This is where all parties go and sign documents and hand over the deposits for the new houses. My solicitor called me and arranged a time for me to go in and sign, I was excited about this…i thought.

It was the thoughts of a brand new start that might make all of the difference that I needed in life. I could 'move on' as my Dad kept saying, put all of my troubles behind me and forget the shit that had gone on. Looking at the house would make me think of the things that we had done together. You think of stupid things that make you remember, I would look at the light switch that the screws kept coming out of and the times that my wife had nagged me about fixing it.

The stupid light in the toilet that would only come on if you switched the kitchen light on. That's the main problem though; every room had some little quirky tale to remind me about my wife. But no-matter where I was, I would still remember her for all the wrong reasons. It is almost impossible to have a good memory about someone when they have hurt you so much. It is as if during your sleep someone comes and removes all of those good memories and puts all of the bad ones at the front of your mind. I can remember the way that I would try to forget about my wife when I was trying to get to sleep when she first left me. I would drag her through a door that led to a cave. This cave went deep down into a cliff that went down under the sea. When we got to the bottom I would push her into a room and close a huge wooden door and lock it. After climbing back up the tunnel inside the cliff I would lock the top door and then hurl both keys as far as I could out to sea. MAD…. yep but it helped me forget her for a while, at least until I was asleep.

That night before I was expected to 'Tie In' I was sat in my kitchen munching through the delicious culinary delight that I had just pulled out of the microwave, and was aimlessly looking around the Kitchen, this gaze of blankness stayed with me, as I decided to wonder around the house. It was my Sisters house before and all the memories came flooding back to me.

All of the parties and gatherings at the house, the times that I had babysat for my sister, the Sunday dinners that I had eaten there and the times that I had spent with my daughter in it. I can remember the first time that I had seen the house. I thought it was enormous and instantly fell in love with it. It has got so much character and I had bought it from her because of that. I remember thinking I loved this fucking house!!! Tears took over again for some unknown reason and I sat on the stairs crying. I then made a decision and I was definitely going to sell, there were just too many bad memories that overpowered the good. ……. Didn't they.

The next day I went into the solicitors armed with a pen and my chequebook ready to get this done. My solicitor who is a family friend looked pensively and smiled at me,

"Right, lets get this done, it wont take long." He said.

I just sat down and my head was spinning, Don't sell,. Don't Sell, Sell, Sell, Don't Sell, Sell, kept going around and around in my head. I stared in front of me with these thoughts bouncing around in my head and looked at all of the official looking papers that signified hundreds of thousands of pounds, and so many memories. Weird really how a signature can change your life, I know that it is symbolic and its not really the ink on the paper that makes the changes but in another way that ink drying on that paper in your signature makes all of the bloody difference.

Time stopped again for me, this is a feeling that I was now getting used to and just let it run its course. All of the feelings that I had experienced over the past year had all come back again…what do I do?

Some time must have passed because my solicitor looked at me and asked if I need some time, I nodded and gave an inaudible sound which was supposed to be a yes.

Fuck what do I do? Dad, I need help? I even sought telepathic help form my wife, will it all be ok, and would we be able to make a go of it in a new house? FUCK., I could feel my pulse rising and sweat running down my neck. All I could think about was the fact that I loved that bloody house and had dreamed of owning it since the day I first saw it when I visited my sister.

I remember sitting in the lounge and telling her how lucky she was and thinking to myself that I would one day love to own a house as this but never believed that I would be possible. It had a very warm feeling about it, homely and it looked that way too. Everybody that has ever been there always comments on what a beautiful house if was. All of the time and effort that I had put into making it mine, the times that I had painted the rooms different colours, I laughed to myself as I remembered that I had changed the colour in the front room 5 times in the two years that I had been in there. The Garden that I loved to care for, even the bloody tiles on the roof that I had straightened after a bad storm. The leak in the roof, which made a damp patch on my bedroom wall. My house…what should I do? Then I knew what to do.

I called to my solicitor who appeared almost immediately.

"I don't want to sell my house!"

"Ok…" He said. "Would you like me to inform the other parties?"

He spoke so calmly and quietly there was an air of complete understanding in his response. I was so grateful of that. He was going to take care of it all for me.

"Yes please if you wouldn't mind"

As he turned to leave and make the calls I said,

"One more thing…."

"Yes." He said with a half raised eyebrow and expectant look and waited for my answer.

"I want to get divorced!"

No Turning Back!

I couldn't believe that I had actually said that. It seemed to take an eternity for it to come out. Shit Divorce.

We have all heard that word many, many times, and where as we know what it means we don't give it that much thought, only that it is a word. But when it is a word that actually affects your own life, then it seems a much bigger word. You realise what it entails with each pronounced syllable. Divorce. The ending of an agreement made in front of God!!!! Well that was a bloody joke. I started to go over the day at the Church. Why didn't I say no I don't take her to be my lawful wedded wife to love, honour and obey from this day forth, in sickness and in health till death do us part, or

something like that…I should have just turned and said
NO!!!!!

But I thought that everything in the world was
wonderful and great, to me it was, it was the happiest
day of my life at that point and I had no thoughts of
doubt in that church. I wished somebody had been sat
there in that church with a fucking crystal ball then I
wouldn't be sat in a bloody solicitors office feeling
completely shit and that all i had worked for and
wanted was ending. Although I had kept saying it to
myself I really still didn't believe that this was
happening to me. Surely there must be something that I
could do to get her back? What was it? Shit…what do I
have to do?

"Ok…………..so Divorce it is then." He said
quietly, trying to sound very sorry. Again he looked at
me with that expectant look with a raised eyebrow. It
sounded like a rhetorical question but I knew from the
way that he asked the question that he was waiting for
a confirmation.
"Yes"
"Ok if you wait here I'll send in my colleague he is
an excellent divorce expert.

His colleague appeared and at once made me feel
at ease.

"ok, I understand that you want to join the
Divorcee club? Don't worry its quite alright there's
plenty of us, you ready?"

"Yes. As I'll ever be. What do you need from me?
"£180 and answers to a few questions"
"Ok" I stuttered,
" Would you like to do this now?" He asked.
"Yes please…. well at least I think I do…Yes lets do it!" I was starting to shake and knew that this was going to be a horrible experience.
"Ok…. Name and address please…."

It started off with all of the usual mundane questions of address's etc and when and where we were married, where the bands were read. Well this is quite harmless I thought. He was very thorough and talking me through all of the technical jargon which I was trying to listen to and understand but all of his words just seemed to merge together and I really didn't give a shit about what he was saying, all I knew was that I wanted a divorce and I wanted it to be done and dusted but unfortunately you have to wait a long time for it.

Then we got to the sticky bits,
"Ok I need to get some details from you to send to the judge to satisfy her as to why you want to get divorced and then they will decide if there is grounds for divorce before they grant the divorce petition. So I would like you to tell me, what is the reason for divorce."

It sounded so easy for him to say that. Yet I didn't want to tell him. I could feel the lump in my throat bobbing up and down and the possibility that I could at any minute burst into tears. I think that he could sense that and tried to help me out a little bit.

Look I know that this is a very hard thing to do. To sit there and tell me what has happened means that something somewhere has obviously gone wrong. I don't need to know who, what where and why, all I need to know is the bare facts for now, and if we need to we can go into them later. We just have to be able to put a strong enough case forward to explain why you would like to dissolve the marriage. So why don't you start to explain why and we can take it from there.

How could I possibly sum up in a few words what has happened? I wanted somebody to know what a bitch she has been all of the pain and tears that she has given me, the time I sat and waited for her, how I tried to help her because I thought that she was ill. Everyday that I couldn't sleep, or eat. It wasn't fair that I couldn't write all of that. Another thing that really pissed me off was that I had to try and satisfy some stranger that I should be allowed to get divorced, who the hell were they to say weather or not we could get divorced, I bet it was a bloody woman as well. What fucking right do they have to decide weather or not I get divorced. Its none of there fucking business. That really pissed me off.

"Look, we're just not together anymore, we have been separated for over a year now, and I know that we are not going to get back together."

"So we can call it irretrievable breakdown then, that's a start". He was helping me here and I needed it.

The solicitor managed to stay sympathetic to me, but I guessed that it was because he knew me. Normally he would probably sit there and think poor bastard another one that's been screwed around. I know that in a lot of cases it's the MAN that leaves the WOMAN, and I think that people do generalise when divorce is discussed, "So why did you leave her then?" well at least that is how it was, I think that now in this day and age of the nineties that you just can't speculate anymore, its either he left her for her or he left her for him or she left him for her even, nothing is black and white anymore.

Over the next hour or so I had to keep thinking about what reasons that I could give for the breakdown of my marriage, and that is difficult as all you end up thinking about is the good times and how much that you hurt since they have gone and how you would move heaven and earth to get them back. Which was strange because usually all I could think of was the bad things that she had done.

But this is reality and a new start had to be made so I talked with my solicitor who gently probed me for answers. I guess because it was now crunch time I was trying to back out of it inside my head, trying to deny what I should do and what I had to do to end all of the shit.

I can remember that by the end of the conversation he had almost converted me. I began to hate her for all that she had done and was looking forward to divorcing the bitch!!!! Truth is thought that I just couldn't bring myself to telling him about the 'Bread Man'. That was too much of a dig in the heart. So I decided not to tell him about that. The questions do get personal and, I can remember him asking me,

"Did you and your wife still have sex?"

I nearly died of embarrassment, but I wasn't sure if it was because of the question or the fact I knew the answer and I had to tell him that we didn't have sex, well once after my daughter was born. Truth is I would have been accepted into a monastery soon. All I had to do was shave my head and wear a brown robe.

"Well there we go another reason, stopping of sexual communications". He scribbled down.

Then I think that I realised that this had to be done and just poured out my reasons. In the end I think that he stopped me and told me that he thought that he had enough reasons.

Truth is thought that this feeling only lasted a short while, as I left the solicitors I can remember walking down the road speaking positively to myself that NOW is the time to move on, start a new life, I'll easily find someone else, a person that will love and care for me in a way that reflects their love for me. Someone who I can trust and love until we are both old any grey!!...

Then I suddenly remembered that that just doesn't happen anymore in this day and age. People say that there is one soul mate out there for all of us…well I used to think that and was very sure that I had found her, but I guess that she proved me wrong on that one. I think that there will be more than just the one. If you think about it, we live in a very large place 'The World' and there are probably twenty soul mates out there, with the wrong people just waiting for us to find them. God what a load of bollocks I hear you say…well we can all dream. Afterall that's all that I have at the moment so let me have that one will you!

On the way back to the office I suddenly remembered that I had to now tell my 'Wife' as she was for a short while the fact that I wasn't going to sell the house and that I had stated divorce proceedings. In a weird way I was looking forward to telling her the news.

I wanted her to start getting upset and ask if there was a way in which we could stop this thing and try again and had run through the scenario in my head of her asking me if I would take her back even after all that she had done but I knew that that wasn't going to happen, or was it.

Why is it that you always have those little niggling thoughts in the back of your mind that are so submissive and would forgive even the most horrible of sins and accept a new beginning? Well at least I'm not the only one with those thoughts…that I am sure of?

Divorce.

The first thing that I had to do was tell my Parents, they had this look in there eye that was just understanding, and pain which was for my pain, but they as parents always do supported my decision and said that 'Well if that's the way that you want to go then its for the best'. I knew that was true but still didn't want to do it.

Not long after that the inevitable happened and my 'Wife' called to see if the sale of the house had gone through.

"Not really." I said.

"Why…what happened? Did they change their mind after all of this time. Did they pull out?"

"No…i decided no to sell the house to them" There was a long silence.

"Why?"

This was it, my ace up the sleeve, she's bound to ask me to stop the divorce when I tell her about it, she's going to want to meet up and talk about it. I know that she will not want to split up forever. I wonder how she will go about asking me back. Ok here goes....

"Because I have started divorce proceedings against you." This was clearly a difficult thing for her to accept and she was obviously adjusting to her new single status, I waited for the plea's and the promises of a new perfect life together...

"Oh..Ok, so what happens now?" Clearly she didn't have much to say to dissuade me, as she probably knew that I would reject any thing that she said.

"Well you will get instructions through the post, I just need you full address for him to send the paperwork through." With that she gave me the address and the phone call ended!

In some ways I wished that I could have been a fly on the wall at the other end of the phone to see her reaction, but no doubt it wouldn't have been the one that I wanted. She probably got straight on the phone to the 'Bread Man' to discuss celebrating the good news, and they could now get together and get married!!!! BASTARD! I hope one day this shit happens to you and it's a hundred times worse!

The next few meetings with my wife were a bit uneasy, and I let her instigate all of the conversations about the next steps. But she was taking it all very well. Far better than me anyway. I can remember when there was some paper work one day that she had to sign that would finally make it all start rolling and it was a motion that would not stop until the divorce was absolute.

We were in my Garden and I was sat with my daughter whilst she read through the paperwork, there were few questions about the Residency of my daughter, that was the biggest let down that I had to go through in all of this, the fact that my daughter would not be living with me, although we were to have joint custody she would live in the week with my 'Wife'.

I really hated that part it made bits of me die inside, I had asked the solicitor about getting residency for me, but he told me that the judge always sided with the Mother in these cases. That really does suck.. As far as I am concerned the one who leaves and starts shagging someone else should loose all of their rights on that very day. The laws in this country need to be addressed on that point, im sure that there are lots of people out there who agree with me. Unless I could prove that she was a bad mother then I should just forget it.

So as my 'Wife' reflected over the paperwork that would set her free, I played in the garden with my daughter, just waiting for my 'wife' to ask me to talk about it, discuss the future, think about things, and I would have sat there and tried to work it out. But she read on and then casually signed the form.

"There you go then, well at least that's it!!" That was all she had to add.

That was it. Signed sealed delivered I'm not yours......

Everything seemed to move to a new level. Surely there would be some relief for me about all of this shit. Well if there was it hadn't come yet. I wanted her to talk to me about it. Maybe be upset or something. But oh no not her. Mrs Ice Queen simply signed the papers and had no sadness about it atall. Standing there in the garden when she left was weird. I had just put the finishing touches on a marriage that I had always wanted and tried so hard to make it work. Why didn't she try to sort this out? What was going on inside her head? I wanted to know if she was upset in the tiniest of ways. That I think would have made me feel that it was worth something in the end. But she didn't and that almost made it worse. On reflection of our short marriage I tried to figure out what we had got out of this besides a beautiful baby girl. The problem was they would only be my answers and things that I would have said were positive.

The reality of the situation though was that it wasn't perfect, it clearly wasn't what my wife wanted atall. I had failed, or if you kind about it we had failed as a couple. It is hard to get closure on something when the other person involved doesn't give you any reasons. But some people would say that you don't need reasons. Something's just end that way and its nobody's fault. Problem here is though that it was her fault. The real reasons will only be known by my wife. The thing is though she could hardly start stating as to why things didn't work in my direction, as it was her who had the need to sneak off and have an affair. Whichever way I looked at it though didn't make me feel any better. People say that out of all experiences in life we learn and get stronger! Well here maybe is the exception. I think that all rational thinking goes right out of the window when matters of the heart are involved.

At least I have time now to reflect on this and move on. By that I mean that there are no nastier surprises waiting for me round the next corner. All of the shit was out in the open and I now knew where I stood. 'It makes you feel ever so slightly better knowing that and just enough to allow you to move forward.

249

Waiting.

So now all that was left was for a Judge to decide if my marriage was indeed over and that decent provisions had been made for my daughter. I hated the waiting for that bloody bit of paper, a decree nici usually takes 6-8 weeks for clearance, and then you have to wait another 6-8 weeks for it to become absolute.

I would count the bloody days down until that first hurdle was over, eventually the time was upon me, but then the court realised that there was a photocopy of a form in the file and not the original so the case was thrown out and we had to start again. I was furious, all I wanted to do was get this thing over with and hope that it would give me closure on this part of my life. But I had to wait another 8 weeks.

"That's the first bloody time I have ever known this happen in nearly seventeen years" said my solicitor. Well that was just bloody my luck wasn't it. Maybe someone was trying to tell me that I shouldn't be getting divorced???

God how sad am I thinking that Fate was to blame, that's nearly as bad as the Yucca Plant scenario. Fate…ha what a complete pile of shit! Don't you just hate it when everyone tells you that Fate had decided that it just wasn't to be…"No I think that the fact she easily jumped into bed with some arse had something to do with it. Oh Shut-up for Christ sake Fate…. FATE someone once said to me. Bollocks to Fate that's all a load of horse shit. Coincidences are the only reason things happen that are related. I wish all the hippies in the world who talk about fate would just Fate-OFF!

As the time came for the first part of the divorce to be passed I went to the local court to hear the names being read out and wait for the judgement to be able to carry on. My solicitor had told me that this was just a formality and that I didn't have to go as all that they do is read out all of the names of the people involved and make sure that there are no objections. So I went into the courthouse and waited outside the room. There was one other man there standing outside. The clerk of the court eventually opened the door and asked us to enter.

"Right …lets get this over with" said the other man there…I sniggered to myself sarcastically and followed him into the courtroom. We waited only a few moments and we were then asked to stand while the judge entered. We were then told to be seated and the Judge ran through the necessary technical jargon and legal talk to enable her to carry on. Then all she did was read out the surnames of all the couples applying for a divorce. There were 22 couples on that day. I wondered if they had all ended the same way as my marriage. Just as the judge was reading through the names I heard someone running up the stairs and my heart stopped. I thought that I might be my wife to stop all this and beg me to take her back. The footsteps carried on passed the room though. The sound of my name being read out snapped me out of my dreamy state and as she passed me on the list I realised that nothing would stop it now. The judge ended up by saying that we were all allowed to carry on with out divorce petitions. Oh that was nice of them I thought.

Now it was all just waiting for forms to be passed and stamped. Soon the 8 weeks passed and I received notification that the first hurdle was out of the way and now the next 8 weeks were just formalities and I would be divorced soon. I was like a time bomb waiting to explode. I really wanted to just get passed this. Once divorced I would feel better and cleared of all this shit. My wife would become my EX-Wife and maybe just maybe I could learn to get on with things again in my personal life. Of course knowing my luck someone in the court would loose the piece of paper and we would have to start all over again. Come on God give me another kick in the balls…. lets have it while I'm down here on the floor just before I get up again please.

All said and done it went quickly and smoothly, my Ex-Wife accepted all of the things pointed out and agreed with everything. I should have put done adultery but didn't want to and as to why I'm not sure? Maybe it was the humiliation of it all, you know the Alpha male being rejected for a lesser male etc…etc… well whatever, on September the 8th 2000 I was finally divorced!

Now finally I was a free man single and able to go forth and multiply again with the vigour of an eighteen year old on viagra. Yeah come on what's stopping me??

Truth be known I didn't want to be divorced. I thought that there was going to be something that would stop it, maybe she would phone me in tears begging me not to go through with it and take her back accepting her forgiveness, even after all that had happened I think that I would have tried if she had just tried to persuade me? Or would I?

In truth I just didn't know how to feel its just I knew I didn't want divorce but it really was the only way to get out of this situation and get on with what was left for me in the real world. It was a place that I was desperate to get back to yet now just wasn't the time.

Moving On.

I think that I was waiting for that day to come and push aside the crying wreck that my body had become and replace it with my 18 year old self, bursting with life and enthusiasm, someone who was invincible and was ready to take on the world, as if all memories of that Bitch would be taken away. A new life of care free relationships and extra sex.... running around with scores of women hanging off my arms laughing at my jokes, willing to please!

However, that little dream never appeared. When I pestered the clerk at the court to find out if my absolute had been processed on that Friday, I was waiting for that rebirth to start, I waited patiently for her to return. She returned the answer that I had wanted, yes sir the absolute had been stamped by the judge and passed, a copy will be mailed to you next week.

"Can I come to the court now and get it? I asked in disbelief.!"

"I'm afraid not sir as we have closed for the week and all of the post is locked in the post room."

"Ok, never mind I'll wait for it, but thank you for your help."

I can remember the Guy in the office asking me if everything was ok and sorted...

Yes, I said. Trying to force a smile....

"Well you a free single man now...of you go!!"

Yes I suppose I am I thought...single now. Yet I didn't feel any different. Why?

I was waiting for the great release of pressure, no more sadness, no moré crying where was this great feeling of Euphoria?

It wasn't there that is all I knew about it. Everyone was asking me if I was ok and happy? Stupid questions when you think about it actually. The real answer was NO and I still felt exactly the same if not worse! Now we were divorced and that was it, there's no chance of us getting back together now is there. Were no longer attached even if it was just by a word.

The worst part of the whole thing was that. I only got closure on the fact that we were no longer married. Inside I still felt the same pain. I still found myself wanted to be with her and talk with her, have us all back as a family. No this was actually worse as now there is no tenuous link between us…the marriage thing was holding on to all possible relationships…then I would suddenly be slapped in the face with the fact that she had been shagging someone else. There that's closure for you!

My life now had to change and slowly each day it did. I got used to the idea that I wasn't going to get back together with my Ex-Wife now and she had her own separate life. Yet this was very weird. I only had my daughter and myself to be concerned about now so I focused on that. It was a weird feeling not having to worry about my ex-wife. Who was going to worry for her? Come on like I gave a shit…. the Bread man will do that. So why did I feel so uneasy about it.

I had to be strong for My Daughter. She is now the single most important thing in my life and I know that she always will be first; nothing will get near that relationship. Her future was the light at the end of the tunnel for me, as long as she was ok then I would be happy, I didn't need anything else. I hated waiting for the times when her mother would drop her off.

I had shut the door on her mother; I was a new person, a very happy and proud father. Eventually I found that people stopped asking those awkward questions about what happened and accepted things. You do realise very quickly who your friends are in times like these, and then you too also understand the meaning of true friendship and love. But these parameters are very short. Its wonderful how protective people can be when a loved one is hurt or in pain.

The human touch albeit emotionally of a tactile sense is a wondrous thing that we should all exercise a little more. If you think about the times that you have kicked yourself for not saying or doing something to help someone, even if it is to tell them that you are there for them it does help them to know that someone does care. I can remember that people are sometimes stuck as to what to say, so they make jokes or hug you, these all make you feel very good inside and you know that you have a lot more friends than you remembered.

When we are going through problems our friends and family all tell us that they wish that there was something that they could do to help us, we nod and thank them hoping that there was some miracle they could perform especially in times like these, but we know deep down that no matter what they say or do nothing is really going to help us more than them just being there, as realistically that is all that they can do.

It is a terrible analogy but the pain I was feeling of my Ex-Wife leaving me was one that I could only relate to the death of someone close. I know that losing someone to death is much harder, but when your going through emotional pain, it just reminds you of when you last felt that hurt inside.

Life does go on and that is the only thing that keeps us going, the thought that one day this will all be a distant memory of something that once was. It is and always will be incredibly sad, if there was no sadness then things would never end, but unfortunately that is a concept that we must learn to accept, that we do not live in a perfect world and sad things are always going to happen.

All we can do is learn form each mistake or bad episode in the hope that the next time it happens and it will, that we will be a few steps nearer to understanding why? And have learnt form previous sad episodes. Truth is though they are all so different and affect us in different ways. I suppose we learn to cope slightly better with them, but lets hope that there wont be that many for us to get used to the feelings that they trigger off.

The good thing now was that I was making progress in my life in terms of accepting how things were and that the only way that they would now change was by my intervention. It could so easily have gotten a lot worse for me, and I might have given up and slumped into a mess, but luckily for me I have a fantastic family around me who I know love and care about me a great deal. But for some I guess it's harder because there are people who have very little support and it must be much harder for them.

As long as you understand that there is someone else somewhere far worse off than you, you then look around you and start to appreciate life and start to see the basic things around you that you have missed whilst you had shut off from the normal world. The shutting off is just something that happens automatically, I think and that enables you to deal with the problem that you have at that time, then when you are getting better the mind lets back in other information slowly and you start to laugh at yourself inside of how you used to be. I frequently remember my intimate time with a certain Yucca plant outside in the garden in the pouring rain that is something that I never forget and makes me smile, even now as I write this I'm smiling.

What Next.

The next part of my life wasn't planned in the slightest, I just had to let things take their course and hope for the best, the recent bad times in my life had just taught me that you can rely on nothing in life, absolutely nothing. Don't get me wrong we can all have hopes and dreams and I think that that keeps us all alive inside, just so long as we remember that they can all come crashing down. But that is just a big learning curve that we all must go through at some stage in our lives, and there will be more than one. So I had to let things just run their course.

I had to make up for some lost time in my life and I did feel like I had lost a year of it, to be honest it had seemed more like five.

Had my Ex-Wife told me as soon as she had started seeing somebody else then perhaps I could have gotten over this along time ago, but she was just too selfish for that. One of her friends had said to me after that she was just having her cake and eating it, she was waiting to decide who to be with. Of course had I known I would have given her the answer to that dilemma she had!

I found myself completely pissed off with her friends and family too, purely because there they were not so long ago, all saying how lovely everything was and how happy they were for us blaa blaa...And all of the time they ALL knew that their daughter / friend was shagging another bloke and destroying me. Well I'm sorry but couldn't one of them tried to help, or tell me? I don't understand some people, two faced is too nice of a simile for them,. BASTARDS...there that makes me feel better...BLOODY BASTARDS.... yes and if your reading this then you know who you all are and I sit her in the comfort of knowing that what goes around comes around so it will be your turns soon you two faced Bastard and I just hope that I'm there to see it! (Doesn't that make me sound bitter? Well I guess I am and no amount of therapy is going to make that go away.)

I now concentrated on getting my life in order. I have a little daughter to provide for, for the rest of my life and by god I was going to put everything that I had into making sure that she got that and her Dad became his old self again.

Entering back out into the social scene was what was needed, but to be in a positive mood. I had now put back on all of the weight I had lost and looked normal again and not the half image of me that I was. Friends even commented that I look and seemed much better, I would joke with them and say it's the Divorce, it is the best thing to have happened to me, of course I knew it wasn't but for me at this moment it was working. If your diet isn't working just get divorced you'll soon loose that extra weight.

After a while I started to see a girl and made her understand that I was just looking for friendship and fun, but she was perfectly happy with that and we had a very good time. After about three months I started to like her more than I should have. I think now looking back that it was maybe a substitute for what I had had in my marriage and she realised and that's what scared her. I truly believe to this day that we could have been great for each other, and I guess that she knows that too but it was to early for that to happen to us because of the difficult situation.

She will remain in the back of my mind for a while, for she gave me back something I thought that I had lost, the ability to get close to someone and let them into my life. It is a wonderful feeling to miss someone when your not with them, sadly now its not her but she will always have a special place for showing me that not all women are bitches, some are just lovely! (Whatever.) Who knows one day In the future we may see each other again somewhere and remember how nice it all was but thanks for showing me that not all women are bad.

It did surprise me at how quickly I could have strong feelings about somebody else. But at the time I didn't even think about it. I have always been someone that easily falls for someone and I tell them, sometimes they respond as I had wished and others they run for the hills. I suppose its just that I believe in telling someone that I like them if I do, what is the point of having feeling for someone and not telling them. After all I'm the sort of person who likes it when someone tells me how they feel, maybe that makes me an insecure person, I don't know and wouldn't like to analyse it too much as the results might not be what I like, so I just carry on waiting to find things that I like.

The hardest part about writing all of this down is the fact that I have to re-live it in my head. At this point now I had left this book unfinished for almost eighteen months because of the memories that it has dragged up. I believe that my mind had shut them off to be able to deal with life. I found that when I went back and wrote some more, a few days later I would get upset and end up sitting at home and bursting into tears. WHY?

Well that's a question that I would love to know the answer to. I personally think that it is because this book is my personal therapy. I didn't go and talk to anybody about my problems and so they got stuck inside my head and got buried further and further inside, then toiling the soil of my mind over each time I sat and wrote would bring it all back and it was never released. It's almost like a thorn inside that had got so deep and every now and then I would pick at it and dig it out but kept leaving it half way out, then it would simply get covered up again until the next time.

To be honest I don't think that this thorn will ever go away. Over the past eighteen months I have learnt a lot and moved on but still in the middle of it all I'm trying to dig out that thorn, but for some reason it doesn't want to come out just yet. Some say that with divorce it never ever goes away, you know I am starting to think that way.

But to talk and discuss things that are inside your head or heart is the best way. The emotional problems that we have are always different. I guess there like fingerprints of our inside. Similar to the person next to you but different enough to make us all search for the answer. As my life has moved along since my failed marriage it has taught me a lot of things. I realised how shut off from the world that I had become. Now this was probably because I was totally happy for the first time in my life. I didn't need anything else.

I had my Wife and that was all that I needed. We would sit in together and just 'be'. Now that may sound really boring to some of you and great to others but I was very happy. The good things to come out of my divorce are the newfound relationships that I have discovered that I have with my family and friends. I learned that you can tell them anything and they will help you no matter what is. I could have turned up at any of their houses at any time of day or night and they would have let me in. And they still would to this day.

Life is difficult but also very enjoyable. We are what we are and nobody will ever change that. And to be quite honest I don't think that I would want it any other way. Things like divorce help you realise how precious things in life are. In the overall great scheme of this thing called life we have to keep things in perspective, unfortunately we don't see things that way when we are down and depressed.

Remember that we only have one shot at this and we should make the most of it. It is easy to take things for granted and be too complacent with the way things are in our lives. Some people fear the unknown and would rather put up with the shit that they have. I would say that's not the way to live and have the courage to change all of that for yourself. We are all entitled to a happy life and it is possible to have one. Having the strength to break away form what you know is difficult and very hard. People seem to look at all of the reasons why not to go instead of the main reason why they should.

All put in black and white it seems so easy. Writing it down and reading it out makes sense to us and we get all positive about making a change. Trouble is when that time comes to actually do it that is when people get nervous and decide to settle for what they know. Better the devil you know they say...

Well after all its their life and we can only be there for them if they need us. That's what friends and family are for, support. They often give there opinion which tends to fall on deaf ears however at least we have let them know that they can come to us. Some times all they need is that.

So reading over the pages of this book you will now know how things happened to me. I know that im just one of thousands of men who will have been effected by the breakdown of a marriage, but probably one of the very few who will have written it down to try and help others. I hope that in some way this will have given you an insight into what happens during a break-up and the fact that you do eventually get through it in the end. It is very difficult and there are times when you just want to curl up into a ball and make it all go away, but unfortunately it doesn't help. Trust me I tried it!

So now that I have eventually finished this little tale what is next for me?

God that's a good question. All I hope is that I can now put this in a corner of my mind and leave it there most of the time. There hasn't been a day gone by where I haven't been reminded in some way of my 'Marriage' and the reason for this book but that's because I believe I still haven't let go of it. I have learned to accept it and live with it and each day brings new excitement. In a weird way I have tried to finish this book many times yet keep finding something to add to it. Now this may be because I don't want to finish it as it could finally end all ties with my marriage in my head. And potentially deep down it is possible that I do not want to do that. I know that all the way along I kept finding excuses to hold on to things just in case……

The future now holds untold things for me and I am looking forward to finding out what is around the next corner. I'm very happy in life and very happy with how I got through this.

During the time that I have been writing this book things have changed, I for one have almost got over my divorce and began to get on with life again. My life will however never be the same again. I had once thought that a large part of it a very important part of it had been decided. I had met somebody that I felt completely at one with.

A feeling of being wanted and needed and loved. That was something that I had always wanted. It gives you a feeling inside that you can't create or buy or even pretend. The emotion of love is indeed powerful and when you don't have that in your life you do feel incredibly lonely. Relationships with Family and Friends change to. If only for a while, yet they make you remember how wonderful they can be. You often get a surge of emotion and realise how much you love these people.

To be able to deal with all this pain is not a task that I would challenge anyone to. It is very depressing whilst trying to get yourself back together because in the end you are the only person that can change it. The healing process is long for some of us and long for others. Getting over divorce is perhaps a wish that all who get divorced want granted. For the person who leaves it is easy. They make a decision and move on.

But when they leave and remove the love and dreams of their partner they don't really lose much sleep over it.

Essentially one leaves a love for a new love. I think that is what makes the pain worse. Them leaving you is bad enough but to leave you for another allows you to sit and put pictures together in your head of them together. It's a bitch as they say but life would be too easy if everything were sweet and nice. I know that there are certain people who can get divorced leave a family or loved ones and move on without to much bother.

I used to wish that I had the same thoughts but then realised that those people must have different views on all kinds of love and relationships. Therefore I decided that I'm glad I'm me and wouldn't want to change as I like being me and the way that I am. Too emotional some of you might say but hey that's what enables me to show how I feel.

Divorce will never leave you for the rest of your life and knowing my luck on it even after I die I will probably still be reminded of it everyday. The pain eases and most of the time I forget about it. This year was the second anniversary of my divorce through; I didn't remember my wedding anniversary. A friend said that I had now got over the divorce.

I don't think that is so for one minute but it certainly hasn't got hold of my life as before.

I found myself again which was nice. Meeting up with myself was just what I needed and I was certainly glad to be back with myself again.

Moving on from this point is scary. I have now been single for a little over three years. I have had dates with women and the longest relationship that I had was about five weeks. That was with the girl in Memphis who I mentioned at the start of this book. We had a great time but travelling from London to Memphis was putting a strain on the term long distance relationship to say the least. I had a great time with a great girl who will no doubt read this book and tell me that she told me so. Thanks for the encouragement K.

I guess the reason for my disastrous personal life is because I just haven't met the right person. What does she have to be? Well that is the ultimate question. I know deep down that I'm looking for such a specific woman who will give me everything that my wife gave me when we were first married. It is because I know exactly what I am looking for and therefore don't think that I should have to settle for somebody for the sake of having someone. Its bloody lonely but what's the point of just seeing someone for company. It's nice but its not fair. So my search continues to find my soul mate, as I clearly didn't meet her yet even though I thought that I had. Still it certainly is better to have loved and lost than never to have loved atall. Meeting someone isn't that important to me now. I have the best friend in the world she just happens to be only four years old.

The reason for the book was to try to help men in the same situation as me who were looking for answers to the question "why did she leave me" they leave for all different reasons but the only thing that matters at the end of the day is that they have gone and you have to get over it. That does happen eventually but it is a bumpy ride.

Some people separate and eventually get back together. I know now that I couldn't and wouldn't if there was a chance to reunite with my ex wife. It comes down to trust. I could never ever believe a word she said to me. Every time that she went out alone I would have thoughts niggling at the back of my mind about where she was and what she was doing.

That is no way to live. When my ex wife had decided to come back and try and I had found out about the bread man I just couldn't imagine having sex with her. I thought about it and wanted to but knew that all I would be able to think about was her having sex with him and that would have destroyed the beauty of the sexual relationship that we once had.

If you imagine when you have a marriage and the sexual relationship you have within that marriage, its as if every other sexual partner you ever had doesn't matter. Now and your wife have a sexual history which began with your marriage, almost as if you were virgins, but once you have strayed outside that relationship to go back is just too difficult.

Others can do it but I couldn't and wouldn't. We never did have sex in the two attempts that she made to come back.

Sex in general has been difficult to get back into since all this happened. I think that in some way I have this enormous fear that having sex means pregnancy which means another baby and that would detract from the one stable thing in my life, my own daughter. Thus resulting in my lack of enthusiasm for sex. I know that your going to say hey there's protection you know, and of course I know that but hey its not guaranteed to work as in my case most condom manufacturers haven't figured out the right strength. There either as think as rice paper or as thick as a hose pipe. So on the rare occasions that I have had sex since the hell that I go through afterwards waiting to see if they are pregnant or not just isn't worth the stress. At least this way I have found the ultimate contraception…if only I could just find a way to market it…

Of course women don't understand it…what do you mean you don't want to have sex…but you're a man…come on stop messing about.

Problem is they eventually realise that I'm not messing about and then suddenly get upset and want to know why…they wonder if they have done something wrong or if I don't find them attractive enough….i suppose in the typical world it must be weird for them being with a man that doesn't want to have sex…..still at least they realise for once how they make us feel sometimes….!

Still life isn't all about sex and it has been so rare in my life over the past three years that it really doesn't bother me that much anymore. Its probably the fact that I know they are not the right one and I'm saving myself…ok I know that sounds corny and you think that now I'm just going to far…firstly a man who doesn't want sex is one thing…but a man that is saving himself now for the right woman…oh come on you say…. but there is something in that. And that is not a line written for any women reading this for me to get your sympathy.

For me in the relationship department now I know that soon there will be someone who will just bowl me over and I will fall completely in love with and will have found my true soul mate. She may read this book and identify with me on everything that I have gone through and decide that I need looking after.

So if you did pick up this book and hoped that it might give you some insight into the depths of divorce and how the hell you can get out of it I hoped that it gave you some help and made you understand that there is a way out of this hell hole eventually. You will get out of it believe me, it just takes longer than you think.

There are people who I have spoken to who chose a different line when there relationship broke down and who got there way through it. I am not saying atall that what I have done is an example to the rest. Some people actually get back together after having an affair and end up staying together for the rest of their time. I had thought about getting back with my wife after finding out about her affair but just couldn't get past the thought that she had been with somebody else. Others can get over it and forget about it but I knew that I couldn't.

I sometimes think of what might be if when my wife returned and I hadn't read that letter, then we might still be together today and I would be none the wiser but maybe completely happy. Yes that is a possibility but you could probably of put money on it that somewhere, someday, somebody would have let the cat out of the bag and how would I have felt then?

I don't for one minute regret getting married and wouldn't turn back the clocks as I have the most wonderful daughter in the world and right now she is all that I have.

This book was to help anybody who is alone and stuck in this position. I wished that I had a book like this to read when I was going through all of this. I looked but couldn't find anything. I just hope that if you understand that your not alone at times like these and you can get through it. Having courage and strength to do that will make you get to where I am currently. Content, but single.

Quite a number of people have read this book at its various stages along the way and given me enormous amounts of encouragement to finish it. Some have even already told me that it helped them understand a few things that have happened in their relationships over the years, giving them closure on old wounds. That's exactly what I had hoped it would do. Finishing it off was very difficult and it has taken me two years to complete it. Writing the start and end were the easy parts but the middle bit when I had to remember every detail was very difficult and I had to keep leaving it. Now as I have actually read it from start to finish it was almost like reading someone else's story. Maybe that means that I have dealt with the issues that I had in my head for the past two years and now I can look at relationships as a good thing and give someone a chance and let them in.

There is no magical answer to any of the questions that you or I have about relationships. If they break down through no fault of yours then you have to learn to accept it and get through it no matter what the circumstances are. That is an easy statement to make now that I have finally got through it. Yet reading this book wont get you through it. Time and friends is all that you have to help you. It gets very lonely and makes no mistake it is very difficult.

But there is only a slight consultation that you know other people are going through the same thing everyday. You wont care or think about them, all that you will think about is how shit your life is at the moment and that you want to get back to normal. You do wonder at times if you will ever get through it. Am I over it? Well if not thinking about it everyday and only occasionally thinking about your ex-wife or partner is being over it then maybe I am. I don't think that you ever truly get over something like a divorce because after time you still miss them. You wonder off into the depths of your mind and dig up the old memories of how wonderful things used to be and how happy you were. I don't think that you should ever forget such a big thing in your life, as it will always remain an important thing.

If my ex-wife ever reads this book then I would like her to know that I do still think about us and the "What could have been" but things change and that is life.

So what is next for me in this wonderful game of life? That is a question that I have asked myself many times. I suppose that I have to just take things as they happen. We all agree that life isn't easy and we can't have what we want. It's only the rich and famous that seems to get that but maybe that's just our point of view because we are jealous of what they have. Yet I would settle for just being happy and in a loving relationship. That is something that money just can't buy. We often think that in life money is the answer to all of our problems and we would all love to have the chance to find out but im sure that its not the case.

We all search for the perfect relationship where love conquers all and secretly hope that one day we will achieve this. Unfortunately it seems that these days relationships do not last as long as they used to . Society has changed the way of life. Why is this? Who can we blame? There is no one to blame but ourselves. It could be the fact that as a whole our generation has life far to easy and I think that we can all agree on that. We are always the hard done by one and seem to find plenty of reasons as to why life owes us more than we have. That is just nonsense. Life certainly is easier than it was for our grandparents or even our parents and we should realise that in a more serious way.

Life is about fun and enjoying ourselves. Not just sitting in and mopping around wondering why the world is against you. So get yourself up off your arse and start to enjoy yourself again.

I think now though you have heard enough from me. You may well say that I have Issues to deal with

David Simpson

you may well think that I am emotionally fucked for all eternity and a bitter man. Others might think that I have helped them see exactly what they needed to see but whatever the outcome and no matter what happens to me in the future I now know that I can get on with it now Afterall what is to stop me now that 'the Bitch left'.

About the Author

David Benson was born in Wales in 1970 and is the youngest of four children. He travelled around quite a bit and lived in many different areas of the UK and also in Canada and the Middle East eventually settling currently in Hertfordshire. David began an interesting line of jobs ranging from Scaffolding to working in a flour mill, but happily moved into the world of advertising in the late 80's. Since then he never looked back and joined the successful publishers that his Sister and Father set up in the early 90's where he still works. David has one mail love in his life his daughter, A close second is the relationship he has with his parents and the rest of his family.